DAILY ALIGNMENT

Tools to Balance Your Body, Mind, and Spirit

LUCY BYRD HOPE

SAVIO
REPVBLIC

A SAVIO REPUBLIC BOOK
An Imprint of Post Hill Press
ISBN: 978-1-63758-659-4
ISBN (eBook): 978-1-63758-660-0

Daily Alignment:
Tools to Balance Your Body, Mind, and Spirit
© 2023 by Lucy Byrd Hope
All Rights Reserved

Cover Design by Tiffani Shea

posthillpress.com
New York • Nashville
Published in the United States of America

1 2 3 4 5 6 7 8 9 10

This book is dedicated to you—
to who you are now and to whom you are becoming.

CONTENTS

PART III: SELF-CARE

PART IV: LIFE SKILLS

PART V: SPIRIT

PART VI: ACTIVITIES

FOREWORD

By Ali Levine,
Breathwork Facilitator, Healer, and Author

THIS IS THE BOOK I needed when I first started my spiritual awakening journey!

I love that this book brings you into alignment in so many ways. It's important that you realize the power that lies within you when you are having a hard time, and this book helps you access that power. What I especially love about this book is that it's bite-sized in nature and can be digested very easily. You can either start reading from the beginning, or, if you are curious, look at the chapters and see what jumps out at you and start there. It's all about getting into your own personal alignment, and I believe you feel that just by opening the book. Even for someone like myself, who has found alignment more and more in my own life, I felt this book was very refreshing and had so many new modalities for me to dive into. I tried each of the techniques and came from a newbie perspective on many, as some I had not heard of. Then, others like breathwork that I do daily, I was able to further anchor into from the tips in the book.

I pride myself on being open to unlearning and learning constantly, and I believe *Daily Alignment* really encourages that, which lets you get deeper within yourself. This book is rooted in self-love and vulnerability, which are two powerful components. When you align with self-love, everything changes for you. You access a power you almost forgot was within you. Then, add vulnerability to the mix, and it's a game changer! Talk about love, truth, bravery, and deep work all at once!

So many of the techniques spelled out in this book are anchored in love. I can feel it in my heart and soul. My heart chakra amplifies while reading this book. Not every book does that. The fact that it's called *Daily Alignment* resonates with how aligned I feel with myself and my heart space after reading it. The name itself is a beautiful reminder of how often we need to align!

What does it mean to be in true alignment with yourself? This book answers that question and allows you to go further. Deep down into your soul. The more I experience chapters of this book and try out new techniques, the deeper I get into my own soul work and self-love. There are lessons in many of these healing techniques, and there are perspective shifts that go further than a regular "mindset" book.

How many of us have read a mindset book and it's all the same self-help and self-talk? Good words to use, but frustrating for so many (myself included), because it doesn't actually do anything. This book, however, teaches you how to be aware of your consciousness and what a consciousness shift looks like. For myself on my own spiritual journey, I have learned the more I allow this shift, the more everything else seems to flow and be in alignment. By bringing awareness and mindfulness to challenging days or moments, I am more deliberate in how I deal with them. In this way, I am gaining the wisdom that comes from observing more of my own life and actions, and this book teaches you that gift. Even if you have no idea what alignment is, or what your consciousness even is, this allows you to start that journey. Be curious and honestly have fun with it all, because this book lets you explore so much in such a simple way!

I invite you to be open and vulnerable with yourself as you read *Daily Alignment*. This book holds space for you and for your soul in such a beautifully divine way. To me, everything is energy; that's the way I view life now. The energy of this book captivates me on another level. It fills my soul with a lightheartedness, while also helping me release any darker shadows or lower energies of myself that I need to shed. There is so much goodness to anchor into, and in today's world, that is needed. This book is a gift of pure self-love that you can give to yourself. When you honor your true self and allow the expression and awakening of your soul, a beautiful and magical door opens. Reading *Daily Alignment* turns the knob on that door for you. I only wish I had this book sooner! I send love and openness to anyone starting this soul journey. It's not an easy one to go on, but it certainly is a beautiful one, and one that will change your life for the better. With this book, you can have the daily alignment you so richly deserve in your life.

Wishing you fulfillment in your own journey of alignment!

NOTE TO SELF

RELAX. BE CALM. STILL YOUR THOUGHTS.

If only.

On my wandering, winding path toward inner peace, one expansive hurdle constantly eludes me: this ever-racing mind of mine.

As far back as I can remember, I've had an active mental landscape. As a child, I frequently counted each of my steps and walked in intervals of seven. I outgrew this special quirk, yet subsequently, throughout my life, I have experienced intrusive thoughts, panic attacks, agoraphobia, anxiety, depression, and suicidal ideation.

Complimentary to these mental and emotional patterns lies the fact that I experience life as a clinically highly sensitive person (HSP). As an HSP, the optimal level of arousal in my brain as it relates to environmental stimuli is set at a lower threshold than that of 80 percent of the human population. As a result, when I interact with the world and others, I frequently become overstimulated. My body chemistry changes accordingly, often leaving me feeling distressed. With this sensitivity, I consistently perceive the subtle cues in the energy and environment around me, which is at times a gift and at others a curse.[1]

With these personality foundations in place, my life has been rich with wonder, although often internally painful. For many years, I sought a way to regulate the feelings and thoughts I experienced, and balance my body, mind, and spirit. In doing so, I discovered, learned, and interpreted a plethora of centering techniques from personal experience, literature, counselors, spiritual teachers, family, and friends.

I found relief from these practices, yet generally did not put them to use when I experienced duress. I discovered two reasons as to why written into my DNA.

One: in a triggered state, such as when I experience heightened anger, fear, or anxiety, my amygdala, my brain's center for emotional processing, hijacks many of my higher neurological functions. My amygdala responds to stressors such as these by going into fight-or-flight mode, my body's evolutionary automatic reaction to a perceived threat, real or not, that allows me to react quickly to danger without thinking things through. This disables my frontal lobe, the part of my brain's cerebral cortex that regulates reasoning and decision-making. At this point, my archaic "lizard brain" takes over, and I operate from primitive and survival-based thought processes.[2]

This is a trait common to all humans, as is the second reason: that I have a negativity bias built into my brain. This means that I am hardwired for negative events to have a greater impact on my brain than positive ones, for negative stimuli to register more readily than positive, and to dwell on negative events more often than positive ones.[3] In fact, about 80 percent of the thousands of thoughts I think each day are automatically negative.[4]

Evolutionarily, both of these traits aided our species in protecting ourselves against threats and generally to stay alive. However, combined with society and technology today, such patterns are outdated and can cause anxiety-and-depression-producing frictions in the mind.

The combination of these two wired-in phenomena boils down to this: when I experience triggering states, my higher cognitive functions tend to disable, and my mind tends to focus on the negativity of the experience itself. As a result, when I am triggered, I am less prone to have the cognitive ability to access the techniques that alleviate a triggered state.

How lovely.

Since I found I clearly couldn't depend on my brain to supply the goods when I needed them, I decided to assemble a visual compilation of the techniques I learned. This way, I could find relief, right then and there. I knew I needed to use an extremely easy-to-read format, because in times of internal struggle, I generally could not focus enough to absorb an entire story or digest a traditional narrative. The result was this book, which I initially wrote to myself.

Now, I read from these techniques each morning to align myself with the habits that I want to embrace daily. When I'm experiencing spiraling negative thoughts, a wave of depression, or relentless anxiety, I peruse these techniques to come back to center. I read them in order, pick a specific appropriate one to focus on for the day, or let the book fall open and read the page that presents itself.

I wrote and compiled these tips for myself to have ready in times when I need them, and now I share them with you in case you happen to ever need them.

So here they are. My notes from myself to, well, myself.

Part I

BODY

YOUR BODY IS YOUR HOME. It is the vessel through which you experience all of life. It is your safe space to find refuge in during times of external upheaval.

Ground yourself in your body by invoking your senses. Engage with your sense of sight, touch, sound, smell, and taste to connect yourself to your body and your present experience.

Harness your breath, the life force within you, to bring yourself back to clarity. Take long, full, deep breaths to center yourself.

Connect to your physical body by feeling into each area of it, from head to toe or toe to head. Slowly scan your body mentally, bringing awareness to, relaxing, and releasing your muscles, one by one.

Listen to your body as it guides you continuously, using discomfort as a form of awareness to alert you to check in with yourself and realign.

Seek what you want externally around you—harmony, stability, and balance—first within yourself. Radiate from inside your sacred home what it is that you want to see in the world. Find safety within yourself, and you are safe wherever you go.

LISTEN

Listen to the sounds around you.

Can you label them?

Perhaps you can hear

    birds chirping,
        the wind passing by,
            a distant train,
                the rustling of leaves,
                  the hum of a fan,
                the crinkling of book pages,
            your breath,
        or
    your heartbeat.

Listen for noises far and near,

    outside in nature,
        inside your home,
            and
                within your body.

The silence of stillness behind all sounds
—listen closely—
can you hear it?

Listening focuses your brain on the sensory experience of hearing, thereby removing your brain's attention from your thoughts. Hearing is your fastest sense. This auditory speed helped your ancestors be readily alerted of approaching danger. You recognize a sound in 0.05 seconds, while it takes 0.25 seconds for you to process something visually.[5] You sense the touch of something in 0.50 seconds, and you perceive smell and taste in over a second.[6]

For the fastest sensory method through which to refocus yourself-when your mind is uncentered, tune into your sense of hearing.

BREATHE INTENTIONALLY

Take a deep breath.

Tilt your head back, relax your eyes,
and perhaps sit or lie down.

Focus on your breathing.
Focus on the air entering your mouth,
nose, and filling your lungs.
Focus on the air exiting your mouth,
nose, and emptying your lungs.

Inhale into your diaphragm,
stretch your stomach muscles,
and open up your ribcage.
Exhale by contracting your stomach muscles,
and let your exhale be longer than your inhale.

Place your hand on your belly.
Inhale into your belly and exhale out of your belly.

Place your hand on your heart.
Inhale into your heart and exhale out of your heart.

Inhale and turn to the right and exhale to the right.
Inhale to the right, and turn to the left and exhale to the left.
Inhale to the left and turn to the middle and exhale.

Breathe in through your nose
and exhale out of your nose,
keeping your mouth closed.
Hold your right nostril closed.
Inhale through your left nostril and
exhale through your left nostril.
Hold your left nostril closed.
Inhale through your right nostril and
exhale through your right nostril.
Repeat twice.

Inhale in through your nose
and exhale out of your nose and mouth.
Inhale in through your nose
and exhale out of your nose, mouth,
eyes, ears, neck, and shoulders.
Inhale in through the soles of your feet
and exhale out of the top of your head.
Inhale in through the top of your head
and exhale out of the soles of your feet.
Inhale in through your back body
and exhale out of your front body.
Inhale in through your front body
and exhale out of your back body.
Inhale in through your entire body
and exhale out of your entire body.

Vocalize your breath
by using your voice to tickle the back
of your throat on your inhale,
and exhale with an audible "ha" sound.

Breathe in through your nose for four counts,
pause for four counts,
and breathe out of your mouth for eight counts.

Breathe in through your nose for four counts,
pause for four counts,
breathe out of your mouth for eight counts,
and pause for four counts.
Repeat.

Breathe in through your nose and mouth for eight counts,
pause for four counts,
breathe out of your nose and mouth for ten counts,
pause for four counts.
Repeat.

Breathe in through your nose and mouth for eight counts,
and breathe out of your nose and mouth for ten counts.

> *"Breathe as waves rolling in and out of the ocean,*
> *rhythmically lapsing over and over."*
>
> -DAWN MARIE CUCCARO

> *"Breathe in love, self appreciation,*
> *blessings, abundance, and miracles.*
> *Breathe out dread, doubt, worry, and fear.*
> *Breathe in bravery, health, joy, trust, safety, and balance.*
> *Breathe out stress, tension, trauma, past and future."*
>
> -JIMI MERK

"Inhale the new.
Exhale the old."

-MEGAN SANGIMINO

Deep breathing is scientifically proven to benefit your heart, brain, digestion, immune system, and bodily response to stressful situations; lower your production of harmful stress hormones; and positively affect the pH of your blood and your blood pressure. Deep breathing has been shown to decrease racing thoughts, rapid heartbeat, anxiety and fear. Slow, deep breathing invokes your vagus nerve and your body's parasympathetic nervous system, which lower your heart rate and blood pressure, signaling your body to relax.[7] Deep breathing initiates your lymphatic system and releases toxins from your body.[8]

Breathe fully to continually align your body.
Your breath stokes the flames
of the fire of the life force within you.
Nurture it.

CONNECT TO YOUR SENSES

Engage with your senses in order to focus your brain
on your somatic experience instead of your thoughts.

What can you see, touch, hear, smell, and taste right now?

Play the 5-4-3-2-1 game.

Notice and point out five things around you that you see.

Perhaps focus on the sight of
the grooves of your skin,
the pattern of your clothing,
the color of nearby walls or buildings,
the hues of surrounding trees or flowers,
or
the light coming from the sun or the moon.

Notice and feel four things around you that you can touch.

Perhaps focus on the feel of
your fingers rubbing against this book,
your clothes laying on your skin,
the floor or ground between your toes,
or
the softness of a pet.

Notice and listen to three things around you that you can hear.

Perhaps focus on the sound of
    an air conditioning unit,
        dogs barking,
  or
distant voices in conversation.

Notice and engage with two things around you that you can smell.

Perhaps focus on the scent of
    a fragrant candle,
      or
lotion you are wearing.

Notice and identify one thing around you that you can taste.

Perhaps focus on the flavor or what you last ate.

Grounding techniques such as these bring your mental energy back into your body, grounding you in the present moment. This removes your focus from your thoughts and puts your attention on the moment at hand.[9]

Grounding techniques assist in coping with triggering emotions and negative thoughts, such as worries about your past and fears of your future. Grounding can assist in alleviating anxiety, panic attacks, and post-traumatic stress disorder (PTSD).[10]

"Our physical body is how we interface with the rest of reality,
the five senses like tethers anchoring us to the moment."
    -ISABELLE PIKÖRN

CONNECT TO YOUR PHYSICAL BODY

Mentally scan your body.

Relax your temples, open your mouth, and allow your jaw to hang.

Slowly move your attention through each part of your body
from your toes to the top of your head.
Observe how the different areas of your body feel.
Step back and witness what sensations arise
without adding judgement or resistance.

Take a deep breath in and out.
Continually breathe in and out
while you envision shading your body in with a pencil slowly from

    your heels to
        your soles to
            your toes to
                the top of your feet to
                    your ankles to
    your calves to
        your shins to
            your knees to
                your thighs to
                    your hamstrings to
    your quads to
        your hips to
            your glutes to
                your pelvis to
                    your spine to

your lower back to
    your upper back to
        your intestines to
            your stomach to
                your chest to
your heart to
    your shoulders to
        your arms to
            your elbows to
                your wrists to
your hands to
    your fingers to
        your neck to
            your throat to
                your chin to
your teeth to
    your gums to
        your tongue to
            your lips to
                your cheeks to
your ears to
    your eardrums to
        your nose to
            your eyes to
                your eyebrows to
your temples to
    your forehead to
        the top of your head to
            the sides of your head to
                the back of your head.

Mentally scan your head as a whole.

Mentally scan your lower body as a whole.

Mentally scan your upper body as a whole.

Mentally scan your front body as a whole.

Mentally scan your back body as a whole.

Mentally scan your entire body as a whole.

Studies show decreased stress levels in individuals regularly performing body scans according to biological markers like reduced cortisol levels and a decrease in the cortisol to dehydroepiandrosterone (a hormone produced in the adrenal gland) ratio. Body scans provide a quick and easy way to reduce stress.[11]

PAUSE

Pause anytime your body has an unplanned physiological change.

Unscheduled changes in your body such as
quickened breathing, heart racing,
sweating, and overall discomfort
can be viewed as objects of awareness
that alert you to check in with your state of being.

Practice SAIN.
SAIN means health in French.
It also serves as an acronym to
Stop, **A**ccept, **I**nvestigate, and **N**on-Identify
as it relates to your mental and emotional experience.
Stop immediately if you are triggered.
Accept the emotion or thought you are having at the time.
Allow it to exist as it is.
Next, investigate the feeling.
Where does the feeling show up in your
body? What does it feel like?
Is your gut churning, your throat constricted,
or are your legs clenched?
Does it cause a sudden hot or cold temperature
change in your body,
for your vision to blur, or for you to see red?
Noting the aspects of your experience can create space
between it and you.

After investigating your mental and emotional experience,
allow the thought and feeling to pass through.
Non-identify with and detach from the emotion or thought.[12]
Exhale and release the feeling.
Inhale and refill with the feeling of mental and emotional balance.

Practice HALT.
Ask yourself, am I **Hungry, Angry, Lonely,** or **Tired?**
If you are any of these, wait to act on big decisions.
After you are no longer hungry, angry, lonely, or tired,
reevaluate and reexamine the situation.
After pausing, you may come to healthier conclusions
and take more stabilized actions.[13]

When you are triggered, whether the threat is real or perceived,
the amygdala in your brain responds as if there is a danger.
Your amygdala signals your body to enter fight-or-flight mode
by emitting the neurotransmitter "corticotropin-releasing
hormone," which prompts your sympa-
thetic nervous system by way of
your spinal cord. This causes your adrenal glands to emit
the hormones epinephrine and glucocorticoids, which help your
body be ready for fight or for flight.[14]

When your fight-or-flight response is triggered, your pupils may
dilate. A dilated pupil lets more light hit your eyeball, resulting in
a better view of your environment, which is helpful when scanning
your surroundings for danger. Your skin may become pale or flushed.
The flow of blood to the parts of your body that can best assist you
in a dangerous situation—your muscles, brain, legs, and arms—is ele-

vated, so accordingly the flow of blood to surface areas of your body is lowered. Your body also increases its capability to clot so that, in case you are injured, your blood loss would be lessened. Your heart rate and breathing may become rapid. These areas are elevated in order to assist the body in its movement by having readily available oxygen and energy. You may begin to tremble as your muscles are ready for movement, which can result in shaking.[15]

If you are experiencing any of these symptoms, acknowledge that your fight-or-flight response has kicked in—and pause.

Once your fight-or-flight response has been triggered, you are primed to react instead of respond in regards to your subsequent actions and language, which can result in yelling, fighting, or other destructive behaviors. Pausing disrupts your body's stress responses and enables you to assess your circumstances rationally.[16]

> *"The reality is that you can't control what happens to you.*
> *You can only control yourself through self-*
> *mastery of your responses...*
> *If you can master this approach, your emotional intelligence*
> *and soft-skills will improve drastically—*
> *and so will your relationships."*
>   -SARAH HODGES

Pause often.

Part II

MIND

YOUR MIND IS THE LENS through which you see the world. The world that you experience is actually the world that you perceive, and your thoughts are the foundation of this perception.

Harness the power of your thoughts. Bring awareness to your thought patterns, styles of thought, and mental cycles. Learn to be the director, conductor, and guide of your thoughts, rather than letting them lead you.

Recognize that with every thought you think, you have a choice about what part of you that you nourish. Are you going to use your next thought to feed the part of you that uplifts yourself and others through compassion, love, and kindness? Or are you going to use your next thought to feed the part of you that holds yourself and others back through hate, guilt, and shame?

When given the option to follow a negative thought and create a downward mental spiral, take the opportunity to spiral up instead, by focusing on a general best-case scenario unfolding, a positive outcome resulting, and things working out for you—or simply the possibility of them doing so. Engage with the broad perspective that perhaps everything is happening for your greatest good, exactly the way it is supposed to.

Encourage yourself to think healthy thoughts and make healthy choices as they relate to you, as you are the one being in life that you do have complete control over. Radically accept everything in your life that you cannot control, including other people, places, and things.

Avoid adding to any pain that you experience. Resisting the experience, complaining, and blaming yourself or others only adds to the overall suffering that you feel. It is your choice whether you accept painful experiences or whether you add your own mental suffering to them, thereby doubling the pain. Minor aches and pains in your body can be a signal that you are mentally resisting something in your life. Mentally picture releasing all resistance in your mind and notice how your body feels afterward.

Recognize when you are being judgmental of yourself or others, and let go of that burden. You can spend your life placing yourself in a position of superiority over others by condemning, criticizing, and attacking them. Or you can allow yourself to live free of this burden by simply experiencing life and all it has to offer from a place of observation and equanimity. Acknowledge that you don't know the long-term outcome and ultimate impact of events that are occurring right now, so avoid becoming overly obsessed with the future negativity or positivity of what is transpiring, and experience what is happening instead.

If you are thinking, choosing positive thought patterns can benefit your well-being. However, whenever possible, release all thoughts. Embrace silence and stillness in your mind. Stay in the present moment and avoid following thoughts about the past or the future. Mentally be where you are, right then and there, at any given time. This allows you to soak up and savor all that the Universe is offering you, instead of wasting this same time regretting or fearing.

Each thought that you think is energetic in nature, and that energy travels, affecting everything from your subsequent bodily functions to your ultimate life path. With every thought you think, you become one step closer or one step further from what you want. Choose thoughts that support the person you want to be. Choose thoughts that support the life you want to lead. Choose thoughts that support the world you want to live in, and create that world, starting with your next thought.

BE A LEADER

However you are thinking,
helpful or harmful,
is flowing through your body at all times.
The cells that make up your body
are responding to your mental direction.

What do you choose to tell
your personal cell team of trillions
functioning as one under your leadership?
They are waiting for your direction right now.
Lead them wisely.

> *"What I think and feel influences every cell in my body.*
> *Energy follows thought*
> *and responds immediately to my intentions.*
> *I am a direct reflection of my spiritual state*
> *and how I feel about myself and life in general."*
> -SHAWN FONTAINE

> *"Your cells are listening."*
> -LAURA POUNDS

What do you choose to tell them?

Psychosomatic refers to the connection between your mind and your body. Mental and emotional experiences result in biochemical changes not only in your brain, but also in nearly all the systems of your body.

Events or thoughts that are emotionally triggering stimulate your limbic system. This then causes further responses in your body, beginning with the emission of ligands—including hormones that cause changes in your body chemistry—and peptides. Once peptides are released, they swim outwards, connecting with thousands of receptor cells all over your body. Once they connect, these peptides communicate on a molecular level to your receptors, which, in turn, communicate the information received from the peptide throughout the inside of the cell. The peptide's message can alter your cell extensively. Further biochemical sequences occur as a result, including, but not limited to, the creation of new proteins, cell division opportunities, and the availability of ion channels. Essentially, the activities of your cells, which direct the functions of your body, are greatly influenced by the receptors that bind to their surfaces, and peptides, including those emitted as a result of intense thoughts or feelings, are examples of such influential receptors.[17]

"SPIRAL UP"

-Tiffany Benford

Your mind often spirals downward into worst case scenarios.
As you imagine negative situations that could occur,
you may suddenly find yourself deep in a fearful fantasy.

Any situation, however, has the potential to unfold positively.
Logically, a positive outcome is half as likely as a negative one.

Play the "what if" game with best-case scenarios played out.
Keep outcomes non-specific and eternally general as you do this.

> What if everything is working out for you?
> What if things go other than you
> planned and turn out alright?
> What if what you hope doesn't happen, doesn't happen?
> What if it does happen, and you are still alright?
> What if everything is happening for your greatest good?

> *"'Supposing a tree fell down, Pooh, when we were underneath it?'*
> *'Supposing it didn't,' said Pooh after careful thought.*
> *Piglet was comforted by this."*
>   -A.A. MILNE

An anxiety spiral can start with a triggering event or worry about the past or future. Your mind then interprets your emotions about the situation as an actual threat. This causes your amygdala to initiate your fight-or-flight response, and your brain signals your body to release adrenaline and cortisol, activating your body's sympathetic nervous system. Your brain may then start to be alarmed by the sensations related to the effects of your sympathetic nervous system being triggered, leading to a state termed "hyperarousal." This leads to the production of more fight-or-flight hormones, and the resulting loop becomes an anxiety spiral. Enabling the prefrontal cortex, the part of the brain correlated with higher neurological function, can halt the spiral.[18]

> *"Anxiety essentially invokes aroused emotions, which*
> *cause the amygdala to initiate the fight-or-flight response.*
> *This is achieved on the HPA (hypothalamus-pituitary-*
> *adrenal) axis, a network linking the brain and the stress*
> *glands, and explains why anxiety is a holistic affair,*
> *affecting not just the mind but every part of the body."*
>
> -ISABELLE PIKÖRN

RADICALLY ACCEPT

Practice deep,
    complete, and utter
        surrender to what currently is.

Practice non-resistance.

Practice non-internalization.

> *"You don't have to*
> *agree with or approve of something*
> *to accept it.*
> *You can think, 'It is true.'"*
>   -Barbara Whittemore

Acceptance ends the suffering caused by
resisting what is at that moment.
The sooner you accept the present,
the sooner you have the potential
to move toward a better future.

> *"Que sera, sera.*
> *Whatever will be, will be."*
>   -Italian saying

> *"Studies have shown that therapies incorporating acceptance*
> *reduce suicidality, substance use, anxiety, chronic pain,*
> *and improve relationships and subjective well-being."*
>   -Jenny Taitz

PRACTICE NON-JUDGMENT

Everything can simply be.

Everything does not need
    to constantly be judged and categorized
        as liked or disliked,
           good or bad,
               right or wrong.

You don't need to constantly decide
    whether you approve or disapprove of
        something, someplace, or someone.
           You can focus on experiencing it or them instead.

When you tirelessly pass judgment on everything,
    you praise or condemn from a place of superiority.
        You can let go of this burden
           and simply experience everything you encounter
               as a human on this Earth
                  in this time space continuum.

Your mind automatically screens, characterizes, and classifies each of your experiences. Certain experiences are judged to be "good," so you want more of them. Certain experiences are judged to be "bad," so you oppose them. What experiences are left are judged to be "neutral," so you disregard them. When you are non-judgmental, you stop "doing" anything about what you are experiencing. You don't seek more of anything, oppose anything, or disregard anything. Non-judgement attunes you to the wonder and awe of life, ends your quest for always wanting more, brings about inner peace, and enables you to view situations and events more transparently.[19]

> *"When you remove the reaction to your experience...*
> *you awaken to the reality that the present moment is*
> *whole as it is.*
> *You don't need to do anything or go anywhere to see that.*
> *You just have to be."*
>
> -PATRICK BUGGY

BE PRESENT

Mindfully embrace this moment
as opposed to ruminating about the past or future.
Savor this second. Absorb what is happening now.
Experience the present deliberately.

As you notice that you are preoccupied in thought,
let go of the thought you are having,
and redirect your attention to the present moment.
Let go immediately
because replaying a thought only makes it harder to let go of.[20]

Envision yourself lying on your back
in a field of bright green grass
with sunshine beaming upon you.
Look up at the deep blue sky
and let thoughts float by

                                        like passing puffy clouds.

Look to birds as a prime example of living in the present.
Birds are provided for in the moment
without being weighed down
by concerns of their past nor fears of their future.

Birds fly freely, living fully from one moment to the next.[21]

When you hear birds chirping,
let them bring you to the moment at hand.
Hear them say

> *"Attention! Here and Now! Wake Up!*
> *Attention! Hear and Now! Wake Up!"*
> -ALDOUS HUXLEY

Staying in the now is a skill of focus
that can be developed with practice.
Practice by noticing when you stray
from the present moment.
Take a deep breath, and ask yourself,

> *"Can I be here now?"*
> *Affirm, "I can,"*

and redirect your attention to the moment you are experiencing.

> *"The present moment is the only thing where there is no time.*
> *It is the point between past and future.*
> *It is always there and it is the only point we can*
> *access in time...*
> *Everything that ever happened and will ever happen*
> *can only happen in the present moment."*
> -MYRKO THUM

> *"Whatever the present moment contains,*
> *accept it as if you had chosen it.*
> *Always work with it, not against it.*

Make it your friend and ally, not your enemy.
This will miraculously transform your whole life."
    -ECKHART TOLLE

Being mindfully in the present moment decreases stress and its subsequent health impacts, aids in combatting fear, regret, and anxiety, and helps with coping with pain and dealing with negative emotions.[22]

You are worthy of this moment.
Be in it.

FEED THE GOOD WOLF

One evening, a Cherokee grandson asked his
grandfather to tell him the ways of life.

"My child," the elderly Cherokee man said,
"There is a fight going on inside all of us.
It is between two wolves.

One is evil.
It is anger, envy, jealousy, doubt, sorrow, regret,
greed, arrogance, self-pity, guilt, resentment,
inferiority, lies, false pride, superiority, and ego.

The other is good.
It is joy, peace, love, hope, serenity, humility,
kindness, benevolence, empathy, generosity,
forgiveness, truth, compassion, and faith."

The child asked,
"Which one will win?"

The old Cherokee man simply replied,
"The one you feed."

-Native American Legend

Which wolf are you going to feed?
Decide with your next thought.

AVOID SECOND ARROWS

Buddha once asked a student,
"If a person is struck by an arrow, is it painful?
If the person is struck by a second arrow,
is it even more painful?"
Buddha then explained,
"In life, we can't always control the first arrow.
However, the second arrow is our reaction to the first.
This second arrow is optional."[23]

When a painful life event occurs,
you are struck with a metaphorical arrow.

Your decision to mentally resist, complain, and feel bad about
the first arrow is when you are struck with a second arrow.

The second arrow is completely optional
and is inflicted by you.
It is your voluntary suffering.

If you stub your toe, stubbing your
toe would be the first arrow.
Growing frustrated, complaining, and
becoming angry about it
would be the second arrow.

If you are cut off while driving,
being cut off would be the first arrow.
Growing frustrated, complaining, and
becoming angry about it
would be the second arrow.
If you lose your job, losing your job
you would be the first arrow.
Growing frustrated, complaining, and
becoming angry about it
would be the second arrow.

Instead of striking yourself with a second arrow,
mentally pull out the first arrow
and heal the wound by talking kindly to yourself,
soothing yourself as if you were your own
best friend, child, or partner.

When a pain-inducing life event occurs, ask yourself,

> *"Do I need to shoot the second arrow?"*
> -SUSAN BERNSTEIN

Replace any negative thoughts that arise by repeating to yourself
"First arrow only" or "That is a second arrow thought."

Avoid the second arrow to ease pain, suffering, and reduce negative
reactions such as self-condemnation, overthinking, and complaining.
Avoiding the second arrow develops the psychological skill of
responding instead of reacting. This means that you can view the
event as it truly is, let yourself feel any emotions that arise objectively,

process the event, and even create a plan to move forward more productively.[24]

Nirvana means "no wind" in Sanskrit. If you look at yourself in a body of water, you see your reflection. However, if wind hits the water, the water ripples, distorting your reflection. The wind causes you to no longer see reality as it truly exists. The second arrow response enables you to experience a state of "no wind"—experiencing life with no distortions—a state of nirvana.[25]

PLAY THE "WE'LL SEE" GAME

A Chinese farmer and his family had a horse.
The horse ran away.
The farmer's neighbors heard this and exclaimed,
    "What horrible luck!"
The farmer responded,
    "We'll see."

The horse came back and other wild horses had joined her.
The farmer's neighbors heard this and exclaimed,
    "What wonderful luck!"
The farmer responded,
    "We'll see."

When the farmer's son was training one of the wild horses,
he broke his leg.
The farmer's neighbors heard this and exclaimed,
    "What horrible luck!"
The farmer responded,
    "We'll see."

The army came through town, demanding
all the men in the town go
to war. Since his leg was broken, the farmer's son could
not be recruited.
The farmer's neighbors heard this and exclaimed,
    "What wonderful luck!"
The farmer responded,
    "We'll see."

The men came back from the army with gold and riches.
Since his son was not in the war, the farmer received none of these.
The farmer's neighbors heard this and exclaimed,
    "What horrible luck!"
The farmer responded,
    "We'll see."

Robbers came to the farmer's town,
stole the gold, and killed everyone who possessed it.
The farmer stood there with no one to
tell him how fortunate he was.
He looked up at the open sky and said,
    "We'll see!"[26]

Events, unto themselves, can be viewed as neither good nor bad. You can remain centered by not following the extremes, since you will not know until the long run whether something was actually positive or negative, and perhaps nothing actually can indefinitely or infinitely be determined positive or negative. So instead of spending time in the extremes, actively live life and let it unfold in front of you without constantly assessing the good or bad inherent in each experience. Only time will tell the impact, ultimate ending, and true purpose for everything.

When an event occurs that makes you uncomfortably heightened in your emotions or thoughts,
replace any extreme responses by saying to yourself,
    "We'll see."

In this story, the principle of equanimity is displayed. The farmer's neighbors are consistently reactive—they encounter stimuli and react according to the state of how events seem, instead of how events actually exist in the broader, clearer picture of time. The farmer, on the other hand, displays equanimity. No matter what event occurs, he does not waste his time neither fearing nor celebrating conclusions based on the events he experiences.[27]

Cognitively, equanimity results in reduced reactivity, higher distress tolerance, and hedonic neutrality (equanimity neutralizes the tendency that no one thing will make you happy indefinitely, and after a while, you get used to things and require something new). Equanimity creates impartiality toward others and lowers prejudice against others.[28]

Equanimity can also increase cognitive flexibility, a marker of positive psychological health and a managing tool for triggering emotional circumstances. This means that best-option responses can be chosen in difficult circumstances, reducing the likelihood of using maladaptive, habitual thought patterns to make decisions.[29]

CHOOSE WHAT YOU THINK

When you notice you are not feeling well,
mentally, emotionally, or physically,
notice what thought you are having at that moment.

You begin to realize negative feelings in your body occur
when negative thoughts are active in your mind.

When you are not feeling well,
ask yourself,
    "What am I thinking about?"

Since whatever it is doesn't result in a good feeling,
you can tell yourself,
    "I don't want to think about that."

Now, ask yourself,
    "What do I want to think about?"

As you actively look for what you want to think about,
a landscape of options presents itself internally and externally.

Would you like to think about:

    what best case scenarios can unfold right in front of you today
    what ways in which you can show yourself you love yourself
    what you are grateful for that is in your line of sight
    the sounds you notice all around you
    the views of the panoramic picture of life surrounding you
    the feel of whatever is touching your toes?

Be an active participant in choosing what you want to carry with you in your mind and choose the thoughts that feel good.

Choosing what you think can be a part of cognitive therapy.

Cognitive behavioral therapy teaches "healthy thinking" by focusing on thought (cognitive) and action (behaviors). By practicing this skill, you can learn to change your thinking patterns and reduce distorted thinking by noticing when you have a thought, disengaging with negative, discouraging thoughts, and engaging with accurate thoughts of self-encouragement. This enables you to feel better, better care for yourself, better cope with life situations, increase time management, reduce and better deal with anxiety and depression, and lower stress.[30]

EMBRACE SILENCE

Instead of thinking about
    how much you think,
        or
    how much you don't want to think,
        or
    how you wish you could stop thinking so much,

what if you used the room in your mind

    to "think" about silence,
        to "think" about stillness,
            and to "think" about inner peace.

A silent mind is one that is connected to source energy—divine energy and energy from a Higher Power. When your mind will not rest, a reset is necessary. This reset not only affects your mind, but also all of the cells in your body as they are affected by your thoughts. This affects your bodily cycles of hormones, sleep, and immunity. The balance in your mind and body that results is homeostasis. Homeostasis can be reestablished in your mind just like it is established in your physical body—by stopping "running." Desist in running around in your mind by inviting silence.[31]

> *"The command center for holistic resetting is at the source.*
> *Be still and know that I am your source."*
> -DEEPAK CHOPRA

Part III

SELF-CARE

CARING FOR YOURSELF PROPERLY PUTS you in a position to live up to your highest potential. Loving, nurturing, and tending to yourself creates solid foundational roots from which you can grow and blossom, allowing you to completely embrace life and all that it is offering you. Giving this type of care to yourself also allows you to fully give this type of care to others. Taking care of yourself is a gift that you give to yourself as well as to the world.

Loving yourself starts with self-compassion. Show kindness, gentleness, and tenderness to yourself. Treat yourself as you would if you were your own child or romantic partner. Positively encourage yourself as if you are your own best friend or support system. Prioritize speaking to yourself in your own loving voice, and not in a voice that mimics someone in your life who may have judged or criticized you.

Mentally, stay focused on yourself, and think about yourself in a loving way. If your thoughts are filled with attempts to control anyone that is not you, you are adding suffering to your life because you cannot control other people. Practice non-comparison by focusing on what you can do to improve yourself and your life instead of what other people are doing or what you feel other people ought to do. Be unapologetically you, regardless of anyone else's thoughts, words, or actions. Don't let anyone else's judgements keep you from being your true self. Remember that what other people think about you is simply not your business.

Recognize that you are always doing your best with the tools and knowledge that you have at any given time, and your best is all that you can do. Know that you are not perfect, as you are human, and that is inherent in your design. You were never meant to be perfect and being perfect does not equate with being lovable. Your imperfections give others permission to be imperfect themselves and create a shared human experience.

Make yourself a priority in your life by honoring your needs and allotting plenty of time and energy to yourself, saying no to anything that does not align with your true self, and setting and keeping boundaries. Build your self-trust by noting moments in each day where you make decisions and choices that benefit your well-being. Live genuinely, speak your truth, and be willing to listen to other people's truths.

Love with an open heart, knowing that, although being vulnerable may lead to heartbreak, being open is the only way to receive all the gifts the Universe has in store for you. Let go of relationships that don't work and people that you find to be toxic to your health and well-being. Forgive yourself and others to free yourself from resentment, anger, and bitterness.

Monitor your emotions and use them to guide you. Let negative emotion alert you to pause and re-align. When anything triggers you, disturbs you, or upsets you, let the wave of intense feelings and thoughts that may arise pass before you make big decisions or approach the person who was the catalyst to your distress. Communicate your feelings and thoughts in love and kindness, as opposed to in aggression or silence.

Be your own caregiver and parent yourself with love, support, encouragement, understanding, patience, and kindness. The relationship that you have with yourself is the most important human relationship you will ever have.

KNOW YOU DID YOUR BEST

When you begin to worry over past events,
tell yourself,

    "I did my best."

It may not have come out how you wanted it to.
Since you could only do the best you could
with the tools and the knowledge that you had at the time,
you did your best.

When you begin to worry over present events,
tell yourself,

    "I am doing my best."

It may not be going how you want it to.
Since you can only do the best you can
with the tools and the knowledge that you have right now,
you are doing your best.

When you begin to worry over future events,
tell yourself,

    "I will do my best."

It may not come out how you want it to.
Since you will only do the best you can
with the tools and the knowledge that you will have at the time,
you will do your best.

"You can do your best and it can still be messy."
-Tiffany Benford

Do the best that you can and release the outcome.

Acknowledging that "you did your best" raises your levels of self-compassion. High levels of self-compassion have been shown to help you be kind as opposed to critical of failures that you make, acknowledge common humanity and that all humans fail, and adopt a healthy approach to negative emotions you encounter when you fail by letting yourself feel the emotions without allowing them to take over. In individuals with high levels of self-compassion, studies have shown a higher drive for self-improvement, and a higher likelihood to report living authentically (living aligned with your true self). Living authentically, in turn, has been shown to increase motivation and develop a growth mindset. Someone with a growth mindset, as opposed to a fixed mindset, sees personality attributes and talents as changeable and growable, making them likely to strive to make improvements in their life.[32]

PRACTICE NON-PERFECTIONISM

Perfect is not your goal.

    You are not perfect
        and
            you are not meant to be perfect.

No longer expect perfectionism from yourself.

Accordingly, no longer expect perfectionism from others.

"Expectations [for perfection] are premeditated resentments."
   -AL-ANON

If you make what you perceive to be a mistake
or wish that you had behaved or acted differently,
review your intentions.
Were they were kind and loving?
You are not necessarily in control of results and outcomes,
but you are in control of your intentions.

To reduce perfectionism, change the ways you think about yourself. Accept your imperfection, note your efforts instead of your results, remove the equation of perfection with lovability, and foster a safe place in which being imperfect is rejoiced, because it means in and of itself that you are human, like we all are.[33]

Making a mistake doesn't mean you are wrong.
Making a mistake means you are human.
Mistakes connect you to your humanity.
How you deal with those mistakes connects you to your divinity.

Reframe your perceived flaws.
The wabi-sabi concept in Japanese culture refers to
the broken pottery pieced back together with gold lacquer
that is worth more than the unbroken pottery.

> *"Imperfection is beauty, madness is genius and it's better*
> *to be absolutely ridiculous than absolutely boring."*
>   -MARILYN MONROE

> *"Perfectionistic tendencies have been linked to a laundry list*
> *of clinical issues: depression and anxiety (even in children),*
> *self-harm, social anxiety disorder and agoraphobia, obsessive-*
> *compulsive disorder, binge eating, anorexia, bulimia, and other*
> *eating disorders, post-traumatic stress disorder, chronic fatigue*
> *syndrome, insomnia, hoarding, dyspepsia, chronic headaches,*
> *and, most damning of all, even early mortality and suicide.*
> *There are studies that suggest that the higher the perfectionism*
> *is, the more psychological disorders you're going to suffer."*
>   -SARAH EGAN

PRACTICE SELF-COMPASSION

Show yourself you love yourself every way possible.

Engage in acts of

    self-care toward yourself,
        kindness toward yourself,
          and
            gentleness toward yourself.

How would you soothe yourself right now
if you were your own

    child,
        best friend,
          or
            romantic partner?

Fall madly in love with yourself today.
Say "I love you" to yourself

    in your mind,
        anytime you want a better-feeling thought,
          looking yourself in the eyes in a mirror,
            or making yourself the "you" in a love song.

If you don't truly love yourself, how can anyone else?

Pause in your thoughts.
Ask yourself, "Am I being nice to myself?"
If not, let go of that thought and allow a new, kinder one.

When you are nice to yourself, you increase your well-being,
and since you are a part of the cosmos,
you increase the well-being,
one tiny bit at a time, of the Universe.
Being kind to yourself is being kind to
the Universe and all within it.

> *"Perhaps we should love ourselves so fiercely that when others see us, they know exactly how it should be done."*
> -RUDY FRANCISCO

> *"Research shows that self-compassion has many benefits, ranging from fewer depressive and more optimistic thoughts, overall greater happiness and life satisfaction to greater social and emotional skills and improvements in physical health."*
> -THE BEST BRAIN POSSIBLE

In studies, increased self-compassion
led to higher drive, joy, body
image, self-esteem, and resolve, and decreased
anxiety, depression, and stress.[34]

You are continually given the option
in thought, word or deed,
to choose love or hate of yourself or others.
Choose love.

> *"Let's not plant any seeds*
> *other than seeds of Compassion and Love."*
>   -RUMI

NURTURE YOUR INNER VOICE

Identify the voice in your head.
You can hear the voice by saying "hello" mentally.
Say "hello" inside your head right now.
The voice that you hear is separate from you.
You can hear the voice, so you are not the voice.
This is a case of a subject and an object.
You are the subject perceiving the object,
so you cannot be the object itself.[35]

Play with this concept to get to know the voice in your head.

Once you've identified the voice,
observe it during different parts of your day.

Step back and witness this voice,
noting how consistently it is with you,
how often it comments on your day,
and how extreme it can sound at times.

Become a neutral observer of this voice.

Patiently, curiously, and lovingly,
learn to detach from and guide this voice,
rather than letting it lead you.

ASK YOUR INNER ALLY

*"You have an inner ally and an inner
critic inside your head.
Tell the inner critic,
that stern, tough, voice,
'I hear you.'
Then turn to the inner ally and say,
'What do you have to say about this?'"*
  -Pasadena Villa

Imagine what your caring and friendly inner support system
would have to say to you.

You are doing a great job!
  I love watching you grow!
    You are just right as you are!
      You are uniquely you!

*"The Universe knows you and
the Universe adores you!"*
  -Abraham-Hicks

Self-compassion consists of self-kindness, showing yourself the
same kindness that you would show a best friend; mindfulness, being
in the present moment instead of pondering what you could have or
should have done; and common humanity, acknowledging that we're
all in this together. We all struggle, we all hurt, and we all mess up—

74

because we are all human. Your inner ally allows you to amplify the love that you feel toward yourself, which allows you to amplify the love that you feel toward the whole world.[36]

> *"Through self-compassion, we become*
> *an inner ally instead of*
> *an inner enemy."*
>   -KRISTIN NEFF, PhD

HEAR NEW VOICES

Pause in your thoughts.

If your thoughts are critical,
ask yourself whose voice in your life
you may be mimicking in your head.

The negative voices that you hear in
your head may be based on
opinions and judgements from people in your past,
so let those voices go and get more up-to-date, positive ones.
What would the loving voices in your life have to say to you?

Imagine hearing the kind voice of

    a friend,
        a family member,
            a pet,
    a counselor,
        a spirit guide,
            an angel,
    a fairy,
        a butterfly,
            your Inner Being,
    your Higher Power,
        or
            the Universe.

"The critical inner voice is an internal enemy that can affect every aspect of our lives, including our self-esteem and confidence, our personal and intimate relationships, and our performance and accomplishments at school and work. These negative thoughts affect us by undermining our positive feelings about ourselves and others and fostering self-criticism, inwardness, distrust, self-denial, addictions and a retreat from goal-directed activities."
-PSYCHALIVE

Negative inner voices generally arise from events in your early ages or from your past. You internalize these voices, and they then regulate the way in which you think about yourself. Critical inner voices are not self-serving; instead, they can result in making unhealthy choices, raising your feelings of self-hatred, and leaving you neither motivated to grow nor behave advantageously. Become aware of negative inner voices by noting when you feel negative emotional shifts occurring within you. Then, decide not to listen to the voice in your head at that moment, and instead invite in and connect to a kinder voice of your choice.[37]

KEEP THE FOCUS ON YOU

Who are you thinking about?

If it isn't "you," you are adding suffering to your life.
You cannot control other people.
What other people think about you is not your business.
So, let's get the focus back on you.

> *"Imagine a hula hoop on the floor.*
> *Step into it.*
> *This is the area that you can control in your life.*
> *Everything outside this hula hoop is*
> *what you cannot control.*
> *You can control yourself.*
> *You cannot control other people.*
> *Stay in your hula hoop."*
>
> -Al-Anon

> *"[Higher Power], grant me the*
> *serenity to accept the things*
> *I cannot change [other people, places, and things],*
> *the courage to change the things I can [me],*
> *and the wisdom to know the difference."*
>
> -Reinhold Niebuhr

Focusing on oneself increases self-care and self-reflection, which are linked to numerous health advantages. Focusing on oneself increases one's ability to engage in hobbies and leisure activities, which have been shown to elevate levels of overall well-being. On the other hand, burnout, which can be caused by focusing on everyone but oneself, has been shown to result in depression, physical ailment, heart disease, and musculoskeletal disorders.[38]

PLACE YOURSELF IN PRIORITY POSITION

You are not here on Earth to please others.

You are here to experience life, grow, and create.

Make yourself a priority in your life.

> What are your needs today?
> How can you honor them?
> How much can you live in the moment?
> How much love can you give yourself?
> How much love can you give the Universe?

Making yourself a priority means setting and keeping boundaries, saying no to anything that takes you off your path, and making sure that you have enough time and energy to address your needs. When you make yourself a priority, you are better able to view the steps you need to take to become accomplished and happy in your life.[39]

BE AUTHENTICALLY YOU

Be unapologetically you,
regardless of anyone else's thoughts, words, or actions.
You are equal to everyone else on this planet.
No one is above you and no one is below you.
You are free to live exactly as you wish to live
and not according to how any other
person believes you should.

If you find yourself worrying about
what other humans think,
know that other people are generally not thinking about you,
because they are usually thinking about themselves.
If other people are thinking about you,
it's possible they are thinking about you
in a positive or neutral way.
Since it's also possible people are thinking
about you in any manner,
what if you enjoyed being you, no
matter what anyone else thinks?

What if you knew that yours is the only opinion that matters
when it comes to how you feel about yourself?
What if you didn't let yourself be swayed
by what other people expect from you?
What if you didn't care what anyone else thinks about you?

Remember, everyone is experiencing
their own struggles in life.
You can choose not to take other people's
words and actions personally.

> *"Other people's judgements are not about me.*
> *Judgements tell me about the person doing the judging—*
> *their beliefs, their fears, their needs, their life scenarios."*
> -Dr. Sharon Horowitz

You are worthy inherently because you exist as the person
that you are. You are someone, not something.
Your worthiness is not equal to what you produce,
or the amount of perfect you appear to be,
or how pleased other people are with you.
You are deserving of love, joy, abundance,
and everything you've ever wanted
solely because you exist as you.
The only validation you need is from within.
Being authentically you is your only true job.

Being authentically you means becoming aware of who you are,
removing the parts of you that society instilled in you, and embracing your true self. You don't hide who you are, you don't become the
person other people want you to be, you remove fear of judgement
and you express your full self. Being unapologetically you means that
you are so accepting and supporting of yourself that you feel worthy and whole without needing others to approve of you. Becoming

unapologetically you enables you to live a life that is full of freedom, joy, peace, and satisfaction.[40]

> *"If a man does not keep pace with his companions,*
> *perhaps it is because he hears a different drummer."*
>   -HENRY DAVID THOREAU

> *"To be yourself in a world that is*
> *constantly trying to make you*
> *something else is the greatest accomplishment."*
>   -RALPH WALDO EMERSON

> *"You don't have to prove anything to anyone.*
> *You are the proof.*
> *You were proven when you were created."*
>   -JIMI MERK

BUILD YOUR SELF-TRUST

Increase your self-trust daily by paying attention to
choices you make that support your well-being.

Note every one of your choices of well-being, from
    choosing to take an intentional deep breath to
        choosing to eat a nourishing meal to
            choosing to speak your truth in kindness to
            choosing to align yourself.

State the affirmation:
"I trust myself to make choices that support my well-being."

When you learn to trust yourself,
you may notice you come into contact
with more trustworthy people
and find yourself in more trustworthy situations.

Ask yourself what positive options are available to you today
and use your choices to build your trust in yourself.

FORGIVE

Forgive yourself and forgive others.

Forgive in order to free yourself of
resentment, anger, and bitterness.
These are toxic emotions that
don't hurt the person that you are feeling them toward;
they only hurt you, the person feeling them.

Forgive yourself for your imperfections, your humanness,
and for past occasions when you feel
you hurt yourself or others.

Apologize if you can.
If you can't for any reason, make a karmic apology.
Treat other people you engage with now
in the kind, loving way that you wish you had treated
someone you hurt in the past.

Learn from the past and release it.
You hold onto the past by keeping it active in your
thought patterns, mental-emotional
cycles, and energetic vibrations.
Think about new things, feel into new emotions,
and align your energy with new activities,
and the past can naturally flow out of your experience.

Forgiveness is a gift of freedom that
only you can give to yourself.

> *"All of the love I have given is not wasted. Love is energy.*
> *Love is the language of the Universe. And it always finds*
> *its way back home. The more love I give, the more love I*
> *feel in every cell of me."*
>
> -LUKAS NOTES

BE VULNERABLE

Perhaps your heart doesn't break,
    because yours has broken so many times that—
        reassembled as a whole—
            it should feel rough or jagged.

Sometimes it feels like dark destruction,
    and sometimes like blissful elation,
        but your heart doesn't feel
            like it's full of pieced together edges and corners.

So, perhaps,
    when you take a risk and are vulnerable—
        by loving deeply, opening emotionally,
            or adventuring into the new—
                and your risk results in pain,
                    instead of getting broken,
                        your heart gets smashed.

Then, like a phoenix,
    it rises resolutely from the ashes
        and grows whole once more—
            in order to willingly be pulverized again.

And perhaps that is your gift.

That if you put your heart out there in full capacity,
even if—even when—it gets obliterated,
inherent in that you put it out there,
it grows completely new, and therefore
completely whole, again.

"I think our capacity for wholeheartedness
can never be greater than our willingness
to be broken-hearted."
  -BRENÉ BROWN

Vulnerability increases physical health,
lowers stress, raises life
expectancy, increases self-esteem, and
lowers depression and anxiety.
Vulnerability increases trust, intimacy,
empathy, understanding,
and self-worth, aids us to discover and
meet the people we want
to be in our lives, facilitates teamwork, allows
us to process negative emotions, raises self-
awareness and accountability, and opens us
to growth.[41]

"Vulnerability is the birthplace of
love, belonging, joy, courage, empathy, and creativity."
  -BRENÉ BROWN

RIDE THE EMOTIONAL WAVE

When anything triggers you, disturbs you, or upsets you,
a wave of intense feelings and thoughts may arise.
Once triggered, it takes between twenty and sixty minutes
for your body chemistry to reset to where it was pre-arousal.

During this time, allow yourself to
ride this wave of emotions.

This wave doesn't need to crash over you,
nor do you need to sink under it.
Instead, coast, knowing your thoughts and feelings
at this time don't need to be acted upon because
they are coming from a place of arousal.

During this time, you can replace
automatic negative thoughts
by saying to yourself

    "processing, processing."
      -*SEINFELD*, "THE MARINE BIOLOGIST" (1994)

Follow the calm feelings, centered thoughts, and peaceful
knowledge. That is the sea turtle guiding you.
Avoid the urging, pushing thoughts
you must immediately act on.
That is the shark on your shoulder.

Coast until you feel emotional stabilization and relief.
You find you make it to the other side of the wave over and over.
Once the wave has ridden through, you may
come to more stable conclusions and desire more grounded actions.

"Feel it, don't fight it, and don't fluff it."
-LAURA POUNDS

Feel exactly what the Universe is sending you.
Don't fight it immediately with thoughts of
"This shouldn't be happening. I wish this wasn't happening.
Why is this happening to me?"
Don't fluff it immediately with thoughts of
"This is fine. No worries. This is no problem."

Feel into the middle and simply experience the emotions that have arisen within you—thereby allowing these emotions to surface and pass. Otherwise, you may experience emotional bypassing, where emotions are not properly felt when they arise, are stored in the body, and come up at a later time.

If you are upset, perhaps after receiving
a triggering letter, email, or call,
wait twenty to sixty minutes before you reply or respond
in order to lower your state of arousal
and, accordingly, your regrets.
During this time, take deep breaths, and re-align.

Once you are triggered emotionally, you are primed to react instead of respond. Your body releases hormones that stimulate your sympathetic nervous system, which activates your adrenal glands, producing catecholamines such as adrenaline and noradrenaline. These increase your heart and breath rate, as well as your blood pressure. Once the moment of the perceived threat has passed, your body needs twenty to sixty minutes to arrive back at its chemical pre-arousal levels.[42]

CHOOSE RELATIONSHIPS
OF WELL-BEING

Your healthiest romantic relationships consist of
you and your partner supporting each other,
bringing out the best in each other,
and growing together.

Recognize the cycles of giving and receiving
in your relationships,
and balance them to keep them healthy.

Partners seeking codependency
may be intimidated by, and therefore
try to inhibit, your growth.

Being independently whole on your own
and combining your life with someone who is whole as well
creates an incredible combination of interdependence;
like how the breath and the voice,
both delightful on their own,
can also create a song.

When you decide a relationship is no longer working for you
and you make the decision to move
forward in your life by yourself,
know that the pain, although initially
unbearable, may lessen over time.

Check in with yourself in one week and see
if the pain has lessened. Then, check in with
yourself in one month, and then one year,
and so on, and note if the pain continues to lessen.
Not facing this pain is not worth
living a life that you don't want to live.

After a relationship ends,
list the things that you want in your next partner,
and focus on finding those traits within yourself
and those around you.
Surround yourself with what you want in your next partner,
and you set the stage for them to come into your life.

Realign by dating yourself between relationships.
Use this time to release the past, and reset your intentions
as to what you want in your next relationship.
In this way you intentionally attract
what you want into your life,
instead of unintentionally looping
energetic patterns from your past
into the energetic patterns of your future.

SET BOUNDARIES

Communicate your feelings and thoughts
in love and kindness,
instead of in aggression or silence.

When communicating about boundaries
or emotional subjects,
practice PLISH.

Pause
When you notice your body has changed physiologically,
your breathing is quickened, you feel
flushed or you "see red,"
wait. Pause before you speak again.
Engage in breathing exercises.
Approach the discussion from another angle.
Know that if you feel you are coming from
a defensive or emotionally charged space,
you can always wait and say more later.

Listen Actively
Listen while the other person speaks.
Listen with all your attention without
having a running dialogue
or refute ready or forming in your head.
Seek to understand what the other person said.

Show this by repeating back to them what
they said in your own words,
from a place of compassionate understanding.

Inner Child Connection
Connect to the other person's inner child.
In a way, adults are still little children in bigger bodies,
especially when in an emotional space
and feeling hurt or wounded.
Focus on and talk to the other person's inner child,
allowing you to feel kinder and more
compassionate toward them.

Solution Orientation
List all the solutions you think could be
implemented in this situation.
Look at the scenario from the angle
of "What can we agree on?"

Help
Utilize professional counselors, therapists,
support groups, books,
your Higher Power, and healing energy.

> *"Speak your mind even if your voice shakes."*
> -RUTH BADER GINSBURG

"THINK before you speak.
Is what you are going to say
Thoughtful,
Honest,
Intelligent,
Necessary and
Kind?"
    -AL-ANON

"Say what you mean, mean what you
say, and don't say it mean."
    -OLD SAYING

Healthy boundaries can provide higher levels of self-esteem, mental health, and emotional well-being, help you focus on yourself, clarify your values and beliefs, reduce burnout, and create independence.[43]

Part IV

LIFE SKILLS

NAVIGATING YOUR LIFE WITH DEXTERITY comes with practice—a lot of practice. Like a fine art, training increases your competence and trial and error hone your skills. View your life as an experiment and simply try things and watch what happens. Maintain the role of the neutral observer. Allow events, sensations, and situations to unfold from a place of detached observation. This allows you to remain a witness to your experiences instead of being constantly pulled in one direction or another as a result of what you perceive.

As you recognize something is not for you, pivot and blend. Turn away from what isn't working, recompose yourself, and reintegrate yourself going in another direction. If you feel stuck, do something different. Try doing the opposite of what you've been doing simply to see what happens.

If you feel like things are hitting you all at once and you are constantly being tested, use that as an opportunity to level up. Face challenges head on as they come and watch as you rise to another phase of life where new rewards and opportunities may await you.

Everything passes eventually, so avoid getting caught up in any experience you believe to be negative. What you are experiencing now may be gone before you know it. Envision yourself already in a place where what is bothering you now has passed, and you may arrive at that place before you know it.

Go slow during your day. Honor and revel in the fact that, until you transition from this Earth, your life will never be done. Slow down and enjoy life instead of rushing to complete everything on your to-do list. If you rush to complete that one, another will simply appear. Soak up what life is offering you now instead of trying to get to a future imaginary place where you believe you will be able to find balance. That place can only be a part of your future if you make space for it now.

Look to the infinite wisdom of nature for lessons and examples of how to live. Observe nature's cycles and seasons, knowing that, just like the tree, flower, and bird, we are all subject to the cycles of producing and resting, giving and receiving, living and dying.

Walk the path of balance by monitoring your cycles of thoughts, emotions, speech, nourishment, and sleep. Like a pendulum, each aspect of your life has an ideal natural resting point where it is in balance. When any area of you is swung to an extreme, as you initially seek to balance it, the pendulum within you related to this area may swing to the other extreme. Observe these swings, and over time, harmonize with the natural center balance point of as many of these areas as possible in order to live a balanced life.

Learn from pain, as pain is a teacher. Pain provides opportunity for growth. Pain provides you with lessons that bring about personal transformation. Once you learn from the pain, let it go. Release it after it has served you, as you no longer need it.

Be honest. When you tell the truth, what you say becomes a part of your past, but when you tell a lie, what you say becomes a part of your future.[44] Be honest now, even if that means having a hard conversation, and save yourself from having to clean up a bigger mess full of harder conversations in your future.

Highlight the positive aspects of your day, your environment, and your life. Discover anywhere in your day that you can find a moment of joy, especially in transitions such as walking, showering, or commuting from place to place.

Step back and take a broad view of life, knowing that in the bigger picture of time and space, daily concerns and trials are of little consequence, and what really matters in your life is the growth, connection, and love that you experience. In the broad scheme of things, over millennia, what will truly matter?

Let go of the word "can't." It doesn't serve you. When you feel the urge to say, "I can't do this," try affirming, "I can," and watch what happens. You always have options. When you feel stuck, turn in any other direction than the one you are in, and look for new opportunities to present themselves.

Overall in life, just show up. You don't have to be at 100 percent, perfect, or just right all the time. Some days, showing up means just putting one foot in front of the other.

Learn from the story of the author Anne Lamott:

"Thirty years ago my older brother, who was ten years old at the time, was trying to get a report written on birds that he'd had three months to write, which was

> *due the next day. We were out at our family cabin in*
> *Bolinas, and he was at the kitchen table close to tears,*
> *surrounded by binder paper and pencils and unopened*
> *books about birds, immobilized by the hugeness of*
> *the task ahead. Then my father sat down beside him*
> *put his arm around my brother's shoulder, and said,*
> *"Bird by bird, buddy. Just take it bird by bird."*
>
> -ANNE LAMOTT

This is how you can approach life, one bird at a time, one day at a time. Assemble your dreams block by block. Build your own empire daily. Carry inside you the behaviors you believe in, surround yourself with people that you care about, and set your sights on what brings you the most joy. Walk in that direction every day.

"FOCUS ON POSITIVE ASPECTS"

-Abraham-Hicks

Focus on the parts of
yourself, your environment, your day, and your life
that uplift you, fulfill you, and bring you joy.

Practice basking in the positive aspects
that are available to you now,
no matter how few there appear to be.
This habit of aligning yourself with positive aspects now
builds momentum
and attracts more positive aspects into
your experience over time.

Discover positive aspects throughout your day,
when you wake up—
in the comfort of your bed or the melody of birds
outside your window,
when you walk into any environment—
in the pleasant room temperature or an interesting piece
of furniture,
when you have a conversation—
in the appreciation of the connection or the potential
for laughter,
when you look in the mirror—
in the depth of your eyes or the upturn of your smile,

looking back on your day by journaling—
in the comfortable weather you felt or a flower you saw
and when you go to bed—
in the rhythm of your breath or the safety of being in your body.
Notice and savor moments of joy throughout your day.
Find pleasure within transitions and in the simple things.
Feel the softness of clothes as you do laundry,
embrace the soothing water as you shower,
walk mindfully from place to place,
notice the trees as you drive,
smile at a stranger,
enjoy the caress of the wind,
smell a flower,
or gaze at the moon.

Focusing on positive aspects is a form of gratitude.

Gratitude has been shown to optimize cortisol levels, resulting in improved sleep and lower levels of fatigue and inflammation in the body; raise oxytocin, known to help mitigate the effects of stress and help form bonds with others; release dopamine and serotonin; increase mood levels; and raise the flow of blood to your hypothalamus, an area of your brain that regulates many of your hormones.[45]

PIVOT AND BLEND

You are constantly

    learning,
        unlearning,
            and relearning.

The experience of life is an
up and down,
    sideways,
        back and forth,
            non-linear process,
so don't be surprised
or resist this when it happens.

As you recognize something is not for you,
turn away from what you don't want,
recompose yourself,
and reintegrate yourself going in another direction.

As you move through complex situations,
let go of what does not serve you,
and turn to embrace the new and unknown
that may serve you better.

Say to yourself as you move with agility,

    "I pivot and blend."
        -Tiffany Benford

If what you're doing isn't working, it makes sense to
do something different.
Try doing the opposite of what you've been doing
if you aren't getting the results you wanted.
View it as an experiment.

"If every instinct you have is wrong,
then the opposite would have to be right."
    -SEINFELD, "THE OPPOSITE" (1994)

"You don't need to
let choices overwhelm you,
let them set you free."
    -JOLENE JOHNSON

When you first start living in awareness,
you may notice many things that you
no longer want in your life,
including behaviors, relationships, and careers.
As you pivot away from what no longer serves you,
your life may feel tumultuous.
Hold steady, keep yourself focused
on what you want as these changes unfold,
and let your reality catch up to your new
energetic point of attraction.

Welcome the pivot and blend, as it is a form of transition that
can take you to new heights, present you with new opportunities, and
incite new ideas and dreams. Choosing to pivot and blend makes you
the director of your life. You are the only one who has to live with the

life that you decide to lead, so pivot and blend until your life is the one that you want for yourself.[46]

> "The secret...is to focus all of your energy,
> not on fighting the old,
> but on building the new."
>> -DAN MILLMAN

> "There is a big mix out there, and there's lots of
> different things going on, and there is not one
> way that was intended to be the right way.
> Just like there's not one color or one flower
> or one vegetable or one fingerprint.
> There is not one that is to be the right one over all
> others. The variety is what fosters the creativity.
> And so you say, 'Okay, I accept that there's lots
> of variety, but I don't like to eat cucumbers.'
> Don't eat cucumbers. But don't ask them to be
> eliminated and don't condemn those who eat
> them. Don't stand on corners waving signs
> trying to outlaw the things that you don't like.
> Don't ruin your life by pushing against.
> Instead, say, 'I choose this instead. This does please me.'"
>> -ABRAHAM-HICKS

> "Decide what you want. Do that."
>> -MARY ENGELBREIT

TAKE IT EASY

The Universe is not in a rush.

You are welcome to simply exist.

"You are free to have no goal."
-BARBARA WHITTEMORE

As often as possible,
be soft and be slow
in your movements and ways.

Discover throughout your day anywhere you can take
a leisurely moment.

What if, everywhere you go,
you are exactly where you need to be
exactly when you need to be there?

"Wherever you go, there you are."
-JON KABAT-ZINN

There is no place that you will reach
where everything will be done, complete, or finalized.
There will always be something left to do,
manifestations left to unfold,
and opportunities left to appear.
Avoid rushing around in an impossible attempt to complete
everything right now.

Be easy on yourself, rest when you can,
and when you have a day that calls for it,
envision pushing an easy button for the day.
Avoid burnout by asking yourself sometimes,
"What is the easiest thing I could think about right now?
What is the easiest thing I could do today?"

> *"You are a human being, not a human doing."*
> -JULIE MANN

For today, be.

Slowing down can assist with deliberateness. From a slower pace, you are better able to focus, realize, and carry out decisions and plans related to your best life path. With a slower pace, you are able to be more present in communication and attempt to understand others better, raising your levels of empathy; and also raise your levels of care, attention, and detail to experiences and events.[47]

Slowing down helps you learn to be patient, to accept more, to be grateful, to know that you can make mistakes—as from a slower pace you can rectify mistakes as you go without as detrimental of consequences—to be persistent, and to honor the cycles of our life, just as the Earth does.[48]

HONOR YOUR PACE

Take time to rest and play,
and take time to create and produce.

Shift between these energies with intention.

Anxiety arises when you are resting and playing
yet thinking about creating and producing—
what you will do, when you want to do it,
or how you will get it done.
This depletes your energy, leaving you tired,
so that when creation and production time comes,
you are not able to be effective, and depression can result.

Instead, intentionally rest and play with focus.
After this, you may feel aligned and balanced,
and all of the initial questions you posed
may answer themselves organically.

Honor the time you spend playing
as natural and inherent in your success.
Let go of spending energy
shaming, blaming, or guilting yourself
about the progress of your creations.
Doing so only depletes your energy so that you are
less able to make progress.
Let go of other people's well intentioned
attempts to guide you to
progress according to a pace that works for them.

Only you know your own rhythms, timings and terms.
As you seek to find this balance, you
may make mistakes as you go.
Commend yourself for trying, and
simply try again next time.

Allow time for inspiration,
and allow time for execution.

WALK THE MIDDLE PATH

You can balance your life by balancing each of the areas within you, finding its center point, its natural place of rest, where it is not too far swung to one extreme or the other.

Monitor your pendulums as they pertain to your
thoughts,
emotions,
words,
actions,
nutrition,
water,
and sleep
to lead a balanced life.

Observe the shifts in your pendulums.
When one is swung too far to one side, following physics,
it will swing almost as far back to the other side,
to the other extreme, and then, slowly,
over time, migrate toward center.
Watch your pendulum swing and honor its stages of motion.
The more areas of life in which your
pendulums are balanced,
the more balanced your overall life is.[49]

"Every element within your being
constantly swings between
two opposite extreme states like a pendulum. This
fluctuation is normal as your body strives to maintain
balance. But, if the pendulum swings too far, balance
is lost, problems arise and breakdown is inevitable.
This principle is true at every level of
existence, from the solar systems
to the cells in your body."

    -DON HEATRICK

Your personal pendulums—
including your thought patterns, eating patterns, sleeping patterns,
relationship patterns, mood levels, and emotional states—
oscillate continually between two outer extremes.

When you set the intention to reach equilibrium
between these extremes, you head toward
a balanced and content life along
the middle path and the natural order of things,
known as the Tao.

BE THE NEUTRAL OBSERVER

In life, you are the witness.
Watch everything, events, feelings and sensations,
from a place of observation and open mindedness.
See how much you can let life unfold without interfering.
It's easy to see what's happening in life.
It's unfolding right in front of you.
Events take place and last just as long as they're taking place.
Don't follow the extremes and continually let go.
As you let go, your energy comes back to center.
If you have no preference,
if the only thing you want is to remain centered,
then life unfolds while you simply feel for the center.[50]

"The day unfolds and the mind doesn't say anything."
> -MICHAEL SINGER

"Use every distraction as an object of meditation
and [it ceases to be a distraction]."
> -MINGYUR RINPOCHE

Observing thoughts, emotions, and sensations as opposed to becoming immersed in them and with them allows you to view your
experiences as temporary, ever changing, and different from yourself and who you truly are. In this way, you no longer identify with
these states.

Instead, you create distance and separate yourself from them, resulting in higher states of peace, serenity, and non-reactivity. This activity of decentering, reperceiving, and de-automatization allows one to "step outside of one's immediate experience, thereby changing the very nature of that experience."[51]

TAKE LESSONS FROM PAIN

Pain is for radical transformation.
Pain is a seed from which you can grow miracles.
Pain is an alert to pivot in another direction.

"Acknowledge pain. Accept it.
Forgive pain itself, and forgive yourself for holding onto it.
Appreciate pain. Appreciate what you learned from it.
Release pain. Let it go, as it no longer serves you.
Everything in your life is happening for you, not to you.
Anything that's on your path is put there to be healed."
    -JIMI MERK

When you find yourself ruminating on
past painful stories, say to yourself:

"I recognize the part I played in past stories.
I recognize I am no longer a part of those stories.
And I release them, setting them free like a bird.
I now allow myself to fill with my natural glowing light."
    -THE SOUL SHEPHERD

"Some days you just have to hold on.
Like keeping your feet on the ground
in the middle of a sandstorm tornado.
In the unknown, can you just hold on long enough
until you are blessed by the struggle?
Harness your fear and use it to pull you to faith.
Use it as an opportunity to strengthen
your relationship with your Higher Power.
Things may appear the same as they did before in
a past painful situation, so you may
fear that a painful outcome
will occur, like it did before.
But what if it's going to be different this time?
What if it's going to be amazing?"

-RYAN GIVENS

"Transformation isn't sweet and bright.
It's a dark and murky, painful pushing.
An unraveling of the truths you've carried in your body.
A practice in facing your own created demons.
A complete uprooting before becoming."

-VICTORIA ERICKSON

"No mud, no lotus."

-TAMARA LEVITT

CHOOSE FAITH OVER FEAR

Take love-based action and joy-based action.

Connect with statements of "I love that" over "I fear that."

Base your decisions on incorporating what brings you joy
instead of on pushing away what you are afraid of.

Fear tries to protect you from pain,
but feeling fear about something in
the future causes pain now,
when the fear itself may never come to pass.
Pre-experiencing pain by means of feeling fear now
doesn't reduce the pain that occurs
if what you are fearing happens later.

You don't need fear to protect you from future pain.
You can face any pain
in your life that you experience head on,
regulate your response,
and re-orient yourself in a less painful direction as you go forward.

"What stands in the way becomes the way."
  -MARCUS AURELIUS

*"We always look at the mountains in front of us
and forget the mountains behind us
were just as hard to climb."*
  -MIMI KENNEDY

*"My fears are nothing but my guidance
system that are showing me what I have
to overcome in order to be more connected
and aligned with my true self, and today
I choose to acknowledge and face my fears,
so I can transcend them and be better."*
  -SHAWN FONTAINE

*"You have
walked through fire
survived floods
and triumphed
over demons
remember this
the next time you doubt
your own power."*
  -YUNG PUEBLO

"If it's coming to you, you're ready for it."
  -JIMI MERK

BELIEVE THE IMPOSSIBLE

Pick six "impossible" things that you are deciding to believe, preferably before breakfast.

For example,

I believe in
    sleeping soundly,
        accepting myself,
            starting a new business,
                writing a book,
                    angels helping me,
                        and magic.

You may find that you look back and see many of these to be proven quite possible.

> *"'There's no use trying,' she said: 'one can't*
> *believe impossible things.' 'I daresay you haven't*
> *had much practice,' said the Queen.*
> *'When I was your age, I always did*
> *it for half-an-hour a day.*
> *Why, sometimes I've believed as many*
> *as six impossible things*
> *before breakfast.'"*
>
>   -LEWIS CARROLL, *ALICE IN WONDERLAND*

ASK NATURE

Learn from nature's seasons, rhythms, and flows.

Cycles of life and death, blooming and withering
and reaping and sowing, are all around
you for you to learn from.
Nothing in nature blooms all year, nor
were you meant to always
produce and give. Time to rest and
receive is inherently necessary.

Trees, with their ability to grow, shed leaves, be bare,
and grow leaves once more,
show you how to grow, let go of what no longer serves you,
and begin anew, again and again.

> *"The trees...show us how lovely it is*
> *to let the dead things go."*
>   -ANONYMOUS

Butterflies, who begin life as caterpillars
and then enter into a cocoon phase,
beat their wings against the cocoon in order to open it,
thereby strengthening their wings.
Both of these processes combined simultaneously enable them to fly.
This shows you how to honor your growth stages
and trust in universal timing.

*"Just when the caterpillar thought the world was over,
it became a butterfly."*
    -PROVERB

Animals, who see differently than we do—
bees who see the ultraviolet spectrum,
mantis shrimps who see circular polarized light,
bullfrogs who see infrared light,
none of which we as humans see—
display that there are dimensions to vision that
we as humans don't access.
This shows you that there is so much
more to this world than
what meets your physical eye.

*"The electromagnetic spectrum describes
all of the kinds of light,
including those the human eye cannot see. In fact,
most of the light in the universe is invisible to our
eyes. The light we can see, made up of the individual
colors of the rainbow, represents only a very small
portion [3 percent] of the electromagnetic spectrum."*
    -SPACE TELESCOPE SCIENCE INSTITUTE

You are made from the Earth, and you will return to it.
In the meantime, honor it and its lessons.

*"Nature is valuable not only for
itself; it is also to be revered
as the single most persuasive and
redemptive work of philosophy."*
    -THE SCHOOL OF LIFE, THE LESSONS OF NATURE

The laws of nature are as they are; we did not choose them and we cannot resist them. Just as nature cycles, we also cycle in our rhythms of growing, procreating, and dying. Nature's laws teach us not to take these things personally, as we are all, including the trees, mountains, and clouds, subject to them.[52]

EXPERIMENT

Life can be like a chemistry experiment.
You can try things and simply watch what happens.
You can look out upon your day and think,
what is the experiment going to look like today?

Anything you view as negative or don't
understand at the moment
may be part of a bigger picture where
it is neutral or positive.

You path is meant to have contrast
because any time you discover
what you don't want, you are clearer in
knowing what you do want.

What could currently be seen as
negative may eventually either

   help you know more of what you do want
      from which knowledge you make a better life for yourself,
         be a lesson from which you grow and evolve,
            be a different situation altogether than it appeared
               at the time,
                  or turn out differently in the long run with time.

Ponder a time in your past when something you thought was
negative ended up being positive
and track evidence of this going forward.
Experiment with adopting the overarching view that
everything is happening as it is meant to,
and that you will look back and everything
in your experience now
will make sense to you at some point,
even if that moment is after you transition from Earth.

"All life is an experiment.
The more experiments you make the better."
    -Ralph Waldo Emerson

LEVEL UP

You may feel that suddenly everything is hitting you at once, and you are being tested over and over.

This is your opportunity to level up!

Just like in video games, when the challenges
come one after another,
you can either sit in the corner and let them pulverize you
and be forced to repeat the level,
or
you can stand strong and firm,
face each challenge and the opportunity within it to grow,
and reach the next level and the rewards awaiting you!

> *"To keep our faces toward change,*
> *and behave like free spirits in the presence of fate,*
> *is strength undefeatable."*
> -HELEN KELLER

SET YOUR FUTURE IN MOTION

Your life is made up of trillions of tiny choices.

Like

tiny

steps

on a

ladder,

your next thought can act as a step toward a better future for you,
your next word can act as a step toward a better future for you,
and your next movement can act as a step toward a better future
for you.

Karma can be seen as—
the choice you make now paves the way for your future.

What future do you want to set in motion with your choice now?

If you want inner peace in the future, quiet your mind now.
If you want self-love in the future, speak kindly to yourself now.
If you want a connection with your Higher Power in the future,
connect to them now.
Apply this concept to anything you want to have in your life.

Live your future now.

Be the person you want to become.

Part V

SPIRIT

YOUR SPIRIT, THE BEING THAT animates the physical vessel you inhabit now and departs this vessel when you transition, is connected to a power that is more expansive than you are. The most beautiful aspects of life, including consciousness, purpose, connection, manifestations, miracles, and faith, are all linked to this Higher Power.

Take daily action to achieve your goals, and leave the results and outcomes up to this Power that is greater than you are. Turn your cares over completely to your Higher Power. Focus on today. Start fresh each day as a blank page, letting go of past programmings, past stories, and past events as if you are beginning a new life every morning.

Check in with your energy and the energetic vibrations that you send out to the Universe. Your thoughts, speech, and actions are all energetic in nature. The Universe matches the energy you send out, as you reap what you sow, so only send out the energy that you wish to receive back.

The energy in the choices and thought patterns that you align with now set the stage for your future. If you want a calmer mind in the future, take deep breaths, ground yourself, and quiet your mind now. Apply this toward anything that you want to be in your life, and you set it in motion to be present on your path as you continue to walk it.

Discover your life's purpose and live it. Let what brings you joy and peace guide your way. Appreciate any lessons along the way, as you may later find these lessons were useful in strengthening your skill set and assisting you in fulfilling your life purpose.

Trust in the natural, complex, and stunning unfolding of the Universe. Be patient and appreciate life from a broad perspective and watch as what you need may come into your life right when you need it.

Enjoy the dance of life, gracefully moving from one moment to another, one relationship to another, one career to another, or one home to another. All the while, honor the time you spend alone, as the relationship that you have with yourself and the relationship that you have with your Higher Power are the only relationships that you will have indefinitely.

As a conscious soul in a human body, when you transition from this Earth, you shed the physical, human vessel you are in now, and return to a non-physical, spiritual state. When you leave behind your body, you leave behind your body's masculine or feminine expression. As a soul without masculine or feminine humanizing features, you are free to embrace both of these energies and utilize them throughout your life. Embrace masculine, producing, doing energy, or feminine, flowing, intuitive energy as you best see fit.

Embrace any other energies that may serve you as you go about your day. Align with the energies of joy, laughter, creativity, balance, harmony, or any others that call to you. Breathe in and out energies that serve you in any situation. Breathe in divinity, and breathe out humanity. Receive everything the Universe is offering to you for your greatest good, and let go of everything that no longer serves you. Daydream, aim for your desires, and know that, as long as you are in alignment with your Higher Power, you can achieve anything you set your heart and mind to.

Get to know your Inner Being, the best version of you and your highest self, and ask this version of you to guide you in life. Maintain alignment with your Inner Being internally no matter what occurs externally around you.

Align with the unifying forces of love, compassion, and kindness. Envision being one with all other life. You originate from the same source as all others do, making you unified and one part of a giant whole. You are interwoven with, and therefore equal to, all other life. You are consciousness living in your vessel, just as other humans, animals, and plants are consciousness living in their vessels. Connect to other souls on this level, allowing you to see past the differentiating factors of the vessels you are in. You are here, just like all other spiritual beings, in your physical casing—creating, expanding, evolving, and growing. When you connect with the soul inside of each vessel instead of with the vessel itself, you find much less that separates you and much more that unites you.

CONNECT TO YOUR ENERGY CENTERS

Breathe into your feet.
Breathe up your legs, into your pelvis,
your core, and your base.
Envision tree roots growing up your whole body.
Feel roots extending from the Earth
and reaching, coiling, and planting into you.
You are rooted into the ground.
You are safe, stable, secure, and protected.
Allow yourself to be enveloped by the color red.

Breathe into your lower belly and your lower back.
You are worthy and deserving.
You are healthy and vibrant.
You are creative energy.
You deserve a life of pleasure and abundance.
You are enough, you have enough, you
do enough, and you are whole.
An orange glow encircles you.

Breathe into your solar plexus.
You are in your own personal power, intention, and fortitude.
You are determined, competent, confident, capable,
resourceful, brave, and strong.
Embrace the fiery yellow light surrounding you.

Breathe into the center of your chest.
Feel into your heart.
You are loving, caring, compassionate,
and kind to yourself and others.
Feel the peaceful harmony and love filling your chest,
and breathe into green love.

Breathe into your throat.
You are expressive.
You hear and speak the truth.
In kindness and clarity,
you vocalize your needs, desires, wants, and boundaries.
You communicate through love.
Feel the expression in your throat in light blue waves
and listen for truths.

Breathe into the middle of your eyebrows.
Feel into your intuition.
Feel into discernment, imaginative
impulses, and a sense of knowing.
Allow clear, calm, intelligent knowledge to pour forth.
Feel into the royal indigo light in your mind's eye.

Feel Divine guidance and Universal connection
as it travels from the center of the Universe
into the crown of your head.
Embrace the violet rays all around you.

Breathe in all the colors of the rainbow, from red to purple.
Mentally travel upward from your feet to your head,
and allow your body to fill with rainbows.

The bottom chakras of your seat, sacral, and solar plexus correspond to your basic instincts, needs, and desires. Your chakras travel up
the scale of enlightenment as they travel up your physical body, with
your heart in the middle. The top chakras of your throat, third eye,
and crown of your head correspond to your higher states of being.

> *"Hermeticists and other esoteric philosophers*
> *noticed that every chakra is linked to an endocrine*
> *gland: the crown chakra with the pineal,*
> *the brow centre with the pituitary and*
> *hypothalamus, the throat centre with the thyroid*
> *gland, the heart centre with the thymus gland,*
> *solar plexus with pancreas, sacral chakra*
> *with the reproductive organs*
> *and the base chakra with adrenals."*
> -AZRIEL RE'SHEL

Strengthening your energy centers allows you to develop compassion toward all of life, motivation and drive, higher amounts of
love for life, the capacity to heal yourself, raised levels of worthiness
and acceptance, and higher intuition, clarity, and focus.[53]

MONITOR YOUR ENERGETIC VIBRATIONS

You are an energetic being, made up of
trillions of vibrating atoms.

> "The vibrations of my Being influence the Universe.
> Everything vibrates and is communicating,
> reacting, responding
> and integrating with other vibrating things.
> Once you being to offer your vibrations on purpose -
> now you are in absolute control of your experience."
> -ABRAHAM-HICKS

Your energetic vibrations interact with your environment
and other humans, as they are also made
of trillions of vibrating atoms.

Channel the energy you wish to align with, such
as when you want to feel better, accomplish
your goals, or be kind to others.
Unlimited energies are available to you, including feminine
energy, masculine energy, child energy, creative energy,
solution energy, Earth energy, wind energy, fire energy,
water energy, magical energy, angel energy, divine
energy, and unification consciousness energy.

Recognize what you are and aren't in
control of as it pertains to
yourself and your energetic vibrations.
In life, you are not in control of other
people, places, or things.
However, you are in control of yourself.

Empower yourself by affirming what you are in control of
as it relates to you, as follows:
I am confidently in control of my voice and what I say.
I am confidently in control of my feet and where I go.
I am confidently in control of my emotions and how I feel.
I am confidently in control of my thoughts and what I think.
I am confidently in control of my choices and what I decide.
I am confidently in control of my action or inaction
in all environments.

Maintain, balance, align and re-align
your energetic vibrations consistently.
Self-regulate your energy and master
your response to external stimuli.
When anything in your experience triggers you,
monitor your physical, mental, emotional,
and spiritual response.
Then, channel the energy that can best
serve you in the situation.

BE THE ALCHEMIST

Thoughts can be seen as bubbles of energy.
If a negative thought bubble travels inside your mind,
disengage with the thought,
and envision the thought floating out of your head.
Shine the light of consciousness on the negative
emotion or discomfort, the pain body, that has
now been created by this negative thought.
Irritability, anxiety, fear, and sadness are
all awakening the pain body.
Shine the light of consciousness on
the pain bodies blindingly,
and through alchemy the pain transmutes into joy.[54]

Alchemy turns base metal into gold.
Do the same internally, turning pain into joy.
See yourself as a joy transmutation machine,
taking pain and transmuting it into joy.
Be an energetic alchemist.

"POINT DOWNSTREAM"

-Abraham-Hicks

When you are having an experience
that you are not enjoying,
use your thoughts to redirect your point of attraction
to align with what you do want.

> *"Upstream thoughts are thoughts you have, which,*
> *when you think them you feel the struggle,*
> *the difficulty, the challenge.*
> *Downstream thoughts are the opposite.*
> *They resonate with feelings of ease,*
> *manageability, belief and*
> *gratitude for all that you have.*
> *You know the difference between*
> *upstream and downstream*
> *thoughts because you feel it!*
> *When you think or say something, it*
> *either feels good or it feels bad."*
> -2 FOR JOY

When feeling physical pain,
your thoughts are generally directed upstream,
so try allowing downstream thoughts in order to feel better.

When you notice you feel pain in your body,
instead of engaging with upstream thoughts like
"Ow, that hurts! I can't believe I feel
this way. I'll never feel better,"
you can decide to practice the exercise of
deliberately turning your thoughts downstream, as follows.

By focusing on thoughts of well-being,
my momentum shifts toward wellness.
As I allow momentum to continue in this direction
as it naturally wants to, I feel even better.
By speaking soothingly and encouragingly to my body,
I watch as my resistance to sensations in my body lowers,
allowing more well-being to naturally enter my experience.
By paying attention to my thoughts and
allowing downstream ones,
I am engaging in a process that, in time,
may align me with wellness.
I know my thoughts play a major role in this process.
Just by thinking thoughts of well-being
more often than I used to,
I see the impact that makes in how I feel.
I know that all feelings and thoughts are temporary
and ever-changing.
I know that this, like any sensation, shall
pass, just like it has in the past.
By being on the other side of past feelings now,
I see evidence of this.

I can tell I'm on the path toward feeling better, even
if it's just beginning by doing this exercise.
I affirm that, in their natural state, the
cells in my body are well,
and I let my body catch up to my affirmation in time.
I like using the power of my thoughts to support
my natural well-being.
I'm glad I'm taking the time to align
my thoughts downstream.
It doesn't matter how long ago I started this process,
it only matters that I start it now—and I am.
I can't wait to see how great my path is from here
now that I'm pointed in the direction of well-being.

> *"Any illness, or departure from physical well-being, begins
> at a cellular level—but the overwhelming propensity of
> your cells is that of thriving. All day, every day, your
> cells are reclaiming balance at such refined and subtle
> levels that most people are completely unaware of the
> power and intelligence of their cellular bodies. Focusing
> upon good-feeling objects of attention is the most
> effective way of providing the optimum environment
> for allowing unhindered cellular communication
> and the ultimate thriving of your physical body."*
> -ABRAHAM-HICKS

Practice turning your thoughts downstream with any situation.

MANIFEST

The Universal Law of Attraction is such that like attracts like.

"That which is like unto itself is drawn."
  -ABRAHAM-HICKS

Pay attention to what you are sending out
into the Universe,
because you are like a boomerang.
What you give out, you attract back.

Your thoughts and speech are energetic vibrations
that you send out to the Universe.
Think and speak in a way that accurately reflects
who you want to be and the life you want to lead.
Your mental and emotional energies can follow suit,
your actions can change accordingly,
and in time, you can align with
that version of you, and even live that life.

When there is something in your experience
that you don't like, pause and take a breath.
Ask yourself,
"What does what I don't want
make me now want?"
Turn in the direction of this new desire.
Listen to your internal guidance
by lining up with positive feelings and

thoughts that feel good.
Focus on receiving from the Universe,
letting everything you need
to complete your manifestation come to you.
Appreciate any new contrast that comes your way,
knowing that it sets you up to have more desires,
which lead to more manifestations
which means more dreams come true.[55]

"As you learn to relax, trust the process,
and flow with the natural current of energy in your life,
you will be led, step by step,
to the manifestation of everything that you want...
You live in a complete state of trust with the universe,
confident that you live in a benevolent world,
and everything is always working out for you."
    -THE JOY WITHIN

"Ask for what you want and be prepared to get it!"
    -MAYA ANGELOU

TRUST IN THE UNFOLDING

Be patient, and the Universe will unfold into your life
what you need, when you need it.

Sync with the abundant rhythm and flow of the cosmos.
Observe the fascinating unfolding
of the complex beauty of the Universe.
Trust in universal timing.
Free fall with the cosmos.
Flow with the natural current of the Universe.
Play with the Universal tides of ebb and flow.

> *"Trees don't sit around and worry about forest fires.*
> *The water in the pond doesn't fret over*
> *turbulence it encountered*
> *a few miles upstream.*
> *And I have never seen a butterfly pry*
> *into the affairs of its fellows.*
> *All of creation is going about the business of living.*
> *If I keep my eyes open, I can learn to do the same."*
> -LAURA LEIN-SVENCNER

Leave your life open for the Universe to fill with
magical surprises.
The Universe does not

> check its clock for the time,
> fill up its future calendar,
> or change its mood based on what
> day of the week it is.

> *"We must not allow the clock and the calendar to blind us*
> *to the fact that each moment of life*
> *is a miracle and mystery."*
>
> -H.G. WELLS

Surrender to your Higher Power's divine will and timing.
Take care of now and trust your Higher
Power to take care of the rest.
Let the Universe know that you defer
to their wisdom and expertise.

View life from a broad perspective.
After you transition, in one hundred years, in 1,000 years,
what will matter?
Which parts of your life would you remember?
How would you feel about everything in your life
if it was 1 million years from now?
How would you feel about things
if you viewed them from the perspective of your Inner Being,
your Highest Self, or your Higher Power?

> *"'Trust me, I know what I'm doing.'*
>
> -THE UNIVERSE"

FIND THE RHYTHM

Each physical step you take can be taken in
rhythmic alignment with the Universe.

This rhythm can be found by syncing each
step you take to a musical beat.
Say to yourself,

> *"As I walk, [take a step]*
> *As I walk, [take a step]*
> *the Universe [take a step]*
> *walks with me [take a step]."*
>   -NAVAJO SAYING

Use any song, mantra, or beat you choose.

> If you desire to do something quickly,
> move "swiftly" by moving on beat,
> just with the rhythm at a faster tempo.

Step by step, your life can become a
rhythmic, centered experience.
By controlling your cadence,
you can remain on your own pace, on "island time,"
no matter where you are.

> *"The goal of life is to make your heartbeat*
> *match the beat of the Universe,*
> *to match your nature with Nature."*
>   -JOSEPH CAMPBELL

ENJOY THE DANCE

Visualize life as a dance.

You have different dance partners—
friends, sweethearts, colleagues, counselors—
who come into your life,
and you begin dancing with them—
as a tango, a waltz, a polka, a jive perhaps.

Then you let go of that partner,
dance to the next partner,
and begin a new dance.

At times, you dance alone—
as a solo artist, a ballerina, a break dancer maybe.
Even if you find a partner for the length of this lifetime,
when you pass on,
you may be with yourself as your main dance partner
once more.
So learn to dance stunningly by yourself.
Learn to love your solo shining premiers.

> *"Enjoy the dance of life,*
> *eloquently grasping the hand of a new partner and*
> *gracefully letting go of the hand of a past one,*
> *all the while honoring the time you spend dancing alone."*
> -LAURA POUNDS

LIVE YOUR LIFE PURPOSE

In Japan, your life purpose is honorably
known as your Ikigai.
Your Ikigai combines your passion,
mission, vocation, and profession.
You find what you love, what you are great at,
what the world needs, and what you can be paid for,
and the combination of these things is your Ikigai.

You may find that, unknowingly to you,
the skills you learned on your life path
are for your life purpose,
and only once you have learned those skills
are you given your life purpose.

> *"My soul's purpose is what I'm*
> *meant to do in this lifetime.*
> *What fills me up with peace, joy, love, and excitement*
> *is the way forward,*
> *and the challenges that come my way*
> *are strengthening my will and purifying my spirit."*
>
> -SHAWN FONTAINE

> *"The meaning of life is to find your gift.*
> *The purpose of life is to give it away."*
>
> -PABLO PICASSO

"Nobody else knows your reason for being. You do. Your bliss guides you to it. When you follow your bliss, when you follow your path to joy, your conversation is of joy, your feelings are of joy — you're right on the path of that which you intended when you came forth into this physical body."

-ABRAHAM-HICKS

HONOR TRANSITIONS

You are a conscious soul living in a human vessel,
a non-physical being living in a temporary physical casing.

You are here to love, grow, create, expand, and evolve
throughout this fascinating school of life.

When you transition from Earth,
the consciousness that is you leaves your body.
You leave this physical, human vessel
and return to a non-physical, spiritual state.

When other souls in your experience
transition and leave Earth,
they enter into a non-physical state.

Connect to loved ones who have transitioned
by embracing phrases that honor their continued existence,
such as "I love you" instead of "I miss you."
Let them continue to love you, and continue to love them.

Perhaps they are in a non-physical
form that your human eyes,
with their availability to translate only certain frequencies
and vibrations of light, cannot perceive.
Solely because you cannot perceive of something
from within the constraints and
limitations of your physical body,
doesn't mean it doesn't exist.

*"We are not human beings having a spiritual experience;
we are spiritual beings having a human experience."*
  -PIERRE TEILHARD DE CHARDIN

"Death is nothing at all.
It does not count.
I have only slipped away into the next room.
Nothing has happened.
Everything remains exactly as it was.
I am I, and you are you,
and the old life that we lived so
fondly together is untouched,
unchanged.
Whatever we were to each other, that we are still.
Call me by the old familiar name.
Speak of me in the easy way which you always used.
Put no difference into your tone.
Wear no forced air of solemnity or sorrow.
Laugh as we always laughed at the little
jokes that we enjoyed together.
Play, smile, think of me, pray for me.
Let my name be ever the household
word that it always was.
Let it be spoken without an effort, without
the ghost of a shadow upon it.
Life means all that it ever meant.
It is the same as it ever was.
There is absolute and unbroken continuity.
What is this death but a negligible accident?
Why should I be out of mind because I am out of sight?

I am but waiting for you, for an interval,
somewhere very near,
just round the corner.
All is well.
Nothing is hurt; nothing is lost.
One brief moment and all will be as it was before.
How we shall laugh at the trouble of
parting when we meet again."

    -HENRY SCOTT-HOLLAND

GIVE IT TO YOUR HIGHER POWER

Picture putting your worries in balloons
and filling them with loving energy.
Release them to float up to your Higher Power,
turning them over completely and safely in their care.

Find a box, any type of box, and label
it your "Higher Power Box."
When you find yourself worrying,
write what you are worrying
about on a piece of paper,
and put it in the box.
As you write the worry down,
mentally turn it over to your
Higher Power, and let it go.
As you practice this, you may find that what you
turn over to your Higher Power has
a way of working itself out.

Acknowledge "answered prayers,"
and find comfort in them in times of uncertainty.

CHANNEL YOUR HIGHEST SELF

Ask your Inner Being, the best version of you and your Highest Self,
to guide your thoughts,
lead your responses to your emotions,
and direct your actions.
Let the best version of you show you the way.

> *"There are two aspects to who you are;*
> *a physical being and a nonphysical being.*
> *The nonphysical being, also called your Inner Being,*
> *Higher Self, or Soul, is always with you*
> *and loves you unconditionally.*
> *Your Inner Being is your expanded,*
> *loving, and compassionate self.*
> *It is the wise teacher within you [that]*
> *knows everything about you,*
> *including why you have the challenges you have.*
> *Your Inner Being is the essence of who-you-really-are,*
> *knows no limits, and assists you in*
> *knowing your true identity."*
> -CHRISTA SMITH

Speak to your Inner Being and your Higher Power.
Ask them for help and share with them
the love and the pain that you experience.
Let them guide you and comfort you.

If you don't feel like doing something
you perceive to be hard,
yet you know you want to do it,
let your Inner Being do it.
Show up and let your Inner Being
complete the task through you.

If this was the future, what would you want to look back on and know that you did now? Let your Inner Being guide your response.

"What would the best version of you do right now?"
    -FRANCIS OF ASSISI

"Ong Namo Guru Dev Namo.
I bow to the Divine Teacher Within."
    -GURMUKHI MANTRA

RECEIVE FROM SOURCE

Be a vessel for the Source that you originated from
to work through.
Open your body, mind, and spirit to the energy of love.
Look through Source's lens of harmony, compassion,
and well-being concerning all.
See from the broad perspective of Source
that spans all space and time.

"*[May I be] an instrument of...peace.*
Where there is hatred, let me sow love;
where there is injury, pardon;
where there is doubt, faith;
where there is despair, hope;
where there is darkness, light;
and where there is sadness, joy.
Grant that I may not so much seek
to be consoled, as to console;
to be understood, as to understand;
to be loved, as to love;
for it is in giving that we receive;
it is in pardoning that we are pardoned,
and it is in dying that we are born to eternal life."
    -St. Francis of Assisi

"*The power is within you.*
You are extensions of this powerful Source Energy.
You are literally [Source] expressing in this physical body."
    -Abraham-Hicks

LIVE JUST FOR TODAY

Keep your focus on today.
Let go of yesterday and forget about tomorrow.
Focus solely on what you would like to experience today.

Imagine what positive news, unexpected blessings, and good tidings could come your way today. Open yourself to receive them fully.

If you had one week left on Earth, what would you do?
If you had one day left on Earth, how would you live?
If this was your last hour, last minute, or last moment, what would matter to you?
Prioritize these things in your current experience.

> *"This is a wonderful day. I've never*
> *seen [one like it] before."*
> -MAYA ANGELOU

> *"'What day is it?' asked Pooh.*
> *'It's today,' squeaked Piglet.*
> *'My favorite day,' said Pooh.*
> -A.A. MILNE

BE A BLANK PAGE

Begin anew.

Begin anew each second, each hour, and each day.

Begin anew each thought, each word, and each movement.

Let go of the stories you tell yourself and who you've been.
Life can start anew at any time.
Begin again, brand new, right now.

> *"My mind knows no limits.*
> *My spirit is infinite and eternal.*
> *I no longer fear my future, because I am creating it.*
> *I choose to turn all of the experiences*
> *from my past into wisdom.*
> *And I let [them] all go.*
> *All that there is right now is a blank new page.*
> *No past programmings.*
> *Just me, pure awareness in the field*
> *of infinite possibilities that*
> *has the power and capacity to create new worlds.*
> *I am manifesting everything and anything*
> *I set my awareness, mind and body to.*
> *I am an ever evolving being of light."*
>
> -SHAWN FONTAINE

Part VI

ACTIVITIES

THERE ARE NUMEROUS ACTIVITIES THAT you can engage in to provide yourself with stability, peace, and clarity whenever you need it.

Incorporate foundational activities, such as meditation daily or when triggered, to achieve balance. To meditate, focus on your breath and observe it as you inhale and exhale. Watch your thoughts as they arise, let them go, and return to your breath. Meditate for five to thirty minutes when you are triggered or on a daily basis to create a consistent practice.

Journal when you are triggered or on a daily basis. Detail what you are grateful for, any healthy choices you made, goals you have, or whatever comes to your mind.

Physically, start moving. Skip, run, do jumping jacks, or dance it out. Engaging in physical activities such as these for short times can help reduce stress.

Initiate your Mammalian Dive Response. Cover your nose, cheeks, eyes, and forehead with a cold washcloth, an ice pack, or put your face directly in cold water. This stimulates your body to think that you are suddenly underwater, which causes your blood flow and heart rate to slow, thereby providing you with relief.

Reset your cranial nerve to reduce pain and increase relaxation. Lie on your back, put your hands behind your head, and turn solely your eyeballs as far to the right as possible for one minute, and then as far to the left as possible for one minute.

Activate your autonomous sensory meridian response, a relaxation response in your body that arises when you hear certain tranquil sounds, such as whispers. Whisper to yourself or listen to videos of whispers, baking, crinkling paper, or folding towels.

Utilize the emotional freedom technique, EFT, or tapping. This technique can alter the synapses that are at the core of negative mental-emotional cycles in your mind, helping you feel better. Create a set-up statement around the problem you are experiencing. Use your dominate hand's four fingertips to tap on your other hand's "karate chop" spot. This is the area between the end of your pinkie finger and the beginning of your wrist on the outside of your hand. Then, tap under the top of your head, your eyebrows, the side of your eye, under your eye, under your nose, your chin, your emotional well below your collarbone and above your armpit, your underarm, and lastly, the top of your head again, in that order. Repeat this three times around.

Try Earthing to reduce inflammation and pain and improve your blood flow and energy. Connect with the Earth's natural electric charge by walking barefoot on the ground outside on grass or stone, or use grounding systems such as conductive mats or pads.

Scream it out. Scream loud and long into a pillow or out in nature. Scream out your anger and frustration and anything that no longer serves you.

Experiment with different forms of therapy. Try aromatherapy, using essential oils to calm you and relieve stress. Try sound therapy, using bells, singing bowls, and other music to induce healing. Try crystal therapy, using crystals as conduits for healing. Try chromotherapy, using color therapy glasses to treat ailments. Try seasonal affective disorder therapy, using a light box to reduce seasonally based depression. Try energy healing therapy, using vibrations to clear, straighten, and realign the energetic pathways of your physical and nonphysical body. Try acu-therapy by receiving acupressure or acupuncture. Try massage therapy to reduce stress and muscle soreness, as well as increase relaxation and circulation. Try professional therapy, including individual therapy and group therapy. Try animal therapy, using animals to help you overcome certain conditions. Try inner child therapy, embracing and parenting the child within you.

Nourish yourself. Consume real food and beverages like organic vegetables, fruits, and teas. Engage with the healing properties of water. Drink water, take a shower, or jump in a river. Spend time in a float tank, a sensory deprivation tank filled with water and large amounts of salt that creates natural buoyancy. Learn integrative health through a functional medicine practitioner. These practitioners take into account your entire physical, mental, emotional, and spiritual health and use holistic methods to get to the root causes of diseases. Take care of your home environment and create a safe, clean space to live in. Enjoy the benefits of travel by taking a short day trip by yourself or a longer trip with a group.

Reap the benefits of entertainment and distraction. Listen to soothing music such as binaural beats and Solfeggio Frequencies. Watch a movie, get lost in a show, or read a good book.

Use the plethora of activities at your disposal to heal, mend, relax, lower stress, anxiety, and tension, and rejuvenate, revive, and restore yourself to your place of most balance.

FOUNDATIONS

Meditation

Find a quiet space.
Sit comfortably cross legged or lie down.
Close your eyes.

Focus on your breath.
Watch your breath go in and out of your body.
Connect to your inhales and exhales
physically, mentally, emotionally, and spiritually.

Notice when your mind strays or wanders from your breath experience, and gently, without judgement, return to observing your breath.

For other areas of focus as you breathe:

Listen to anything neutral in your environment,
such as a fan, the rustling of leaves, crickets, or distant voices.

Rub the tips of your fingers on each hand together slowly, one by one.

With your eyes closed, envision and focus upon the image of a bright orange flame.

Repeat a calming mantra, such as, "I am open."

Meditation practice dates back thousands of years. Meditation has been shown to lower and manage stress, raise well-being, peace, and inner calm, raise awareness of the present moment and self-awareness, raise creativity and tolerance, and help shift perspective. Meditation has been shown to assist in mitigating anxiety, asthma, cancer, chronic pain, depression, heart disease, high blood pressure, irritable bowel syndrome (IBS), sleep issues, and headaches. Choose a quiet spot free from disturbances, get in a relaxing position sitting or lying down, and adopt an open awareness, allowing your thoughts to flow through without judging them. Remember, there is no perfect way to meditate, and simply engaging in the practice increases your meditation muscles, so you are always benefiting.[56]

Journaling

List everything in your line of sight for which you are grateful.
Alphabet from "a" to "z" everything for which you are grateful.
Document evidence that things work out for you.
List any wins you experienced.
Write any positive choices you made.
Document synchronicities, coincidences, or signs you observed.
List goals and affirmations to achieve them.
Write what comes into your mind as a stream of consciousness.

Journaling has been shown in studies to lower anxiety and depression, raise immune system response, increase gratitude, help heal from trauma, and raise abilities related to memory.[57]

Movement

Performing intense activity for short periods can alleviate stress.
Actively stretch.
Skip.
Hula hoop.
Jump rope.
Swing.
Garden.
Swim.
Practice yoga.
Do fifty jumping jacks.
Take a walk.
Dance as hard as you can to one song.

Physically get a different perspective on things
by switching up your blood flow.
Lean over and massage your head upside down,
or lie down and put your legs up against the wall.

Note what the movement raises within you mentally and emotionally. Let whatever surfaces rise, feel it, and release it.

Movement raises your general health and state of well-being, releases endorphins—the neurotransmitters that make you feel good—lowers stress and its effects, helps your cardiovascular, digestive, and immune networks, raises self-confidence, mood, and relaxation, reduces depression and anxiety, and benefits sleep.[58]

Mammalian Dive Response

Initiating your Mammalian Dive Response involves stimulating your body to think that you are suddenly underwater, causing your blood flow and heart rate to slow, calming your body and mind.

To stimulate your Mammalian Dive Response:

- cover your nose, cheeks, eyes, and forehead with a cold washcloth

- cover your nose, cheeks, eyes, and forehead with an ice pack

- cover your nose, cheeks, eyes, and forehead with an icy gel mask

- Put your face directly into an ice bath. Lean over, holding your breath, and submerge your nose, cheeks, eyes, and forehead in the bath for 30 seconds.

The Mammalian (in possession of a backbone) Dive Response refers to certain physiological responses in your body that are brought on by submersion in water that overrule your natural reflexes, essentially helping you tolerate a lower amount of oxygen, as you would need to if you were underwater.

The changes that result in your body are:

- Bradycardia, or lowering your heart rate, 10 to 30 percent in the average person

- Peripheral vasoconstriction, or contraction of your blood vessels, which increases blood flow to your brain and heart and reduces blood flow to your limbs

- Triggering of your trigeminal nerve, which occurs when your face, forehead, and nose area are submerged, improving cerebral blood flow

- Triggering of your vagus nerve, which results in the lowering of your pulse

When you experience the inability to think clearly or process information, activate your Mammalian Dive Response. After thirty seconds, higher cognitive processes are accessible, such as problem-solving ability, information processing, and clarity of thought.[59]

*This activity slows your heart rate. Avoid this is you have heart problems or a slow heartbeat.

Cranial Nerve Reset

Move your head side to side.
Rate your level of discomfort.
Lie on your back.
Intertwine your fingers together.
Put your hands behind your head,
against the back of your head.
Feel into the heaviness of your head and feel
your fingers as they hold your head.
Turn solely your eyeballs and look to
the right as far as possible.

Look to the right for up to a minute.
Then, gradually bring your eyes back
to their center resting point.
If you suddenly yawn, sigh, or swallow, gradually bring
your eyes back to their center resting point at that
time (regardless of whether it has been a minute).
Look to the left for up to a minute.
Then, gradually bring your eyes back
to their center resting point.
If you suddenly yawn, sigh, or swallow, gradually bring
your eyes back to their center resting point at that
time (regardless of whether it has been a minute).
Sit up.
Once again, rate your level of discomfort and compare it to your original level.

Resetting your vagus nerve through this exercise has been scientifically shown to provide relief from pain, raise levels of relaxation, and
strengthen social engagement. This activity repositions the vertebra
in your neck referred to as "atlas" and "axis," induces mobility in your
neck and spine, and raises blood flow to your brainstem, which is
where the five cranial nerves relating to social engagement are found.

This increased neck mobility and bloodstream circulation improve
the function of the "ventral branch" of the vagus nerve, which sends
relaxation signals to your body and promotes well-being.[60]

Autonomous Sensory Meridian Response

ASMR, autonomous sensory meridian response, is a relaxation response in your body brought about by hearing calming sounds such as whispers.

ASMR refers to the tingling sensation you may feel in response to specific soothing sounds. It generally starts in your head, shoulders, and spine and extends to other areas of your body, ultimately creating a pleasurable feeling of relaxation. ASMR triggers are different from person to person, and frequently consist of slow, repetitive, quiet, and intimate actions. Personal attention triggers include activities such as hair brushing and whispering. Task-based triggers include activities such as finger tapping, crinkling paper, stirring food, baking, or folding towels.

ASMR has been shown to elevate mood, reduce stress, aid sleep, and reduce pain.[61]

To activate your ASMR, listen to videos of whispers, baking, hair brushing, finger tapping, crinkling paper, stirring food, or folding towels.

Try whispering these affirmations to yourself:

1. I am brave.
2. I am capable.
3. I am supported.
4. I am growing.
5. I am aligned.

Emotional Freedom Technique

Emotional freedom technique, EFT, or tapping,
is a technique that can melt synapses at
the core of painful mental-emotional cycles in your mind,
reducing negativity in your thoughts and feelings.

EFT refers to using your fingertips to tap certain spots on your body while simultaneously concentrating on negative physical or emotional pain. Tapping has been shown to induce your parasympathetic nervous system, rewire your brain to run in healthier patterns, and re-balance the energy in your body. Studies have shown that tapping assists with anxiety, depression, PTSD, fear of public speaking, test-taking, and other phobias, pain, illness, weight control, and athletic performance.[62]

Tapping has also been shown to lower cortisol and stress levels.[63]

> *"Speculation on the mechanisms involved suggests that*
> *tappingon acupoints while a presenting emotional problem*
> *is mentally activated rapidly produces desired changes*
> *in the neurochemistry involved in that problem."*
> -FEINSTEIN, 2012, THE TAPPING SOLUTION

> *"We all collect and store in our minds a series of beliefs*
> *and perceptions about ourselves....These beliefs are really*
> *just thoughts that you've repeated so often that they have*
> *become your reality. Think of a goal you'd like to achieve*
> *in your finances, career, health and/or relationships.*

What limiting beliefs come to mind about
whether or not you can achieve it? EFT helps to
interrupt those repetitive thought patterns."
      -THE TAPPING SOLUTION

To Practice EFT:

Concentrate on the issue you are having.

Create a "set-up statement" around the problem.
A set-up statement acknowledges the issue and
also acknowledges the parts of you that are unconditional.

For example, if you are experiencing anxiety,
your setup statement could be
"Even though I am experiencing anxiety,
I completely, deeply, and utterly accept myself."

Start to tap.
Using your dominate hand's four fingertips,
tap on your other hand's "karate chop" spot—
the area between the end of your pinkie finger and the beginning
of your wrist on the outside of your hand.

As you do this, out loud, say the "set-up" phrase three times.

For round one,
tap five and seven times on the points below in the order they are in
while simultaneously identifying
where the problem shows up in your body and how it feels
physically.

As you do this, out loud, say the "set-up" phrase three times.

For round two,
tap five and seven times on the points below in the order they are in while simultaneously identifying
how the problem shows up in your life and how you feel about it emotionally.

As you do this, out loud, say the "set-up" phrase three times.

For round three,
tap five and seven times on the points below in the order they are in while simultaneously identifying
the neutral and positive aspects of the problem, what progress you are making with it, ways in which you are successfully handling it, and what you may even appreciate about the problem.

Tapping Points:

Your head: using four fingers, tap around the top of your head.

Your eyebrow: using two fingers, tap the inside of your eyebrows. Start from the side nearest to your nose.

The side of your eye: using two fingers, tap the hard area between your eye and temple.

Under your eye: using two fingers, tap the top of your cheekbone.

Under your nose: using two fingers, tap the middle area between the end of your nose and the top of your lips.

Your chin: using two fingers, tap the middle area beneath your lips and above your chin.

Your emotional well: using four fingers, tap the soft space directly below your collarbone and above your armpit.

Your underarm: using four fingers, tap on the side of your body below your armpit and equivalent laterally to your peck.

Your head: using four fingers, tap around the top of your head.

If feelings arise, let them surface. Honor them and truly feel them.

Let them flow through you and release them.

Continue tapping as many rounds as necessary until you feel better emotionally, mentally, and physically.[64]

Earthing

Connect with the Earth's surface electrons.

"Earthing" is connecting your body to the Earth's natural electric charge. The origins of Earthing go back thousands of years. Earthing techniques include walking barefoot on the ground outside on conductive surfaces such as grass, soil, gravel, stone, or sand, or using grounding systems such as conductive mats, pads, body bands, or patches while sitting or sleeping. Earthing connects you to the Earth's natural healing energy, and has been shown to reduce inflammation, pain, and stress, and improve blood flow, energy, sleep, and vitality.[65]

Primal Scream

Scream as loud as you can, as long as you can, from your diaphragm.
Scream into a pillow, or in the shower, or alone in nature.
Scream out your anger, frustration, fear, doubt, and anything that has ever held you back.

THERAPY

Aromatherapy

Use essential oils to send therapeutic scents from your olfactory nerves to the emotional center of your mind, your amygdala.

Aromatherapy is a healing method that uses natural plant extracts to increase health and well-being and enhance physical and emotional health. Aromatherapy has been used for healing for thousands of years, and in ancient cultures such as those of China, India, and Egypt.[66]

Use peppermint oil to help with stomach issues, including IBS symptoms.

Use lavender oil to help reduce stress and provide calming and relaxation.

Use bergamot oil to help reduce stress, pain, and inflammation.

Use chamomile oil to help with sleep and anxiety reduction.

Use ylang ylang oil to help reduce tension and stress.

Use eucalyptus oil to reduce coughs and nasal congestion.[67]

Use the plethora of essential oils available to support your body's natural well-being.

Sound Therapy

Use the high vibrational frequencies of bells, singing bowls, drums, and other music to induce emotional and physical healing by raising your personal energetic vibrations.

Sound therapy has been shown to improve physical and emotional health and well-being, reduce stress, anxiety, depression, blood pressure, pain, cholesterol, heart disease, and stroke, treat post-traumatic stress disorder, dementia, autism spectrum disorder, learning difficulties, behavioral and psychiatric disorders, and cancer, lower risk for coronary artery disease and stroke, and increase memory, sleep, and relaxation. Sound therapy dates back to ancient Greece, where music was used to help treat mental disorders.[68]

Crystal Therapy

Use the Earth's gift of crystals as conduits for healing.

Allow the high-vibrational, positive, healing energies to raise the vibrational frequencies of your energy, thereby releasing unhealthy and negative energy.

Crystals allow higher vibrational energy to flow into your body, causing negative, toxic, and lower-vibrational energy to break apart and fall away. Crystals channel energy and focus on healing your body from the inside. Crystals have certain vibrations and frequencies as a result of their molecular composition. These vibrations and energies interact with your energetic vibrations and work to raise mood and well-being in your mind and health. Crystals can act as magnets, absorbing negative energies and thereby creating space for positive energies. Crystals, products of the Earth itself, harness the energies of the sun, moon, and oceans, all of which are natural healing energies. Crystals interact with your body's energy centers, or chakras, and help balance them. Crystals can increase concentration and creativity and cleanse your physical, emotional, and spiritual bodies.[69]

Chromotherapy

Color therapy, also called chromotherapy, is a method of treating ailments by using colors.

Use color therapy glasses or spend time engaging with certain colors that feel healing to you.

Chromotherapy is a method of healing that has been in use dating back centuries. Electromagnetic radiation, or light, involves the fluctuation of electric and magnetic fields in your environment. The rate at which a matter vibrates stipulates its density and form. Physical matter vibrates relatively slowly, as compared with subatomic matter, or light energy, which vibrates at or higher than the speed of light. Essentially, light is energy, and color itself is a result of the interplay between energy and matter. Each color corresponds to a certain wavelength, frequency, and amount of energy. Each of the atoms, cells, and organs in your body is continually in movement, producing its own frequency and vibrational energy. When the frequencies of the structures of your body vibrate with the frequencies of certain colors, they harmonize, providing cellular balance. Disease or disfunction are indicated when areas of your body are not vibrating at the frequency they normally do. Chromotherapy uses the vibratory rates, wavelengths, and oscillations of specific colors to re-align these unhealthy energy frequencies. Chromotherapy treatments have been proven to assist with anxiety, seasonal affective disorder, circulatory issues, and chronic pain.[70]

> *"Light affects both the physical and etheric bodies. Colors generate electrical impulses and magnetic currents or fields of energy that are prime activators of the biochemical and hormonal processes in the human body, the stimulants or sedatives necessary to balance the entire system and its organs."*
> -SAMINA AZEEMI AND S. RAZA

Seasonal Affective Disorder Therapy

Seasonal affective disorder (SAD) is a specific type of depression that generally occurs annually during the fall and winter.

A light therapy box can help relieve this depression.

SAD lamps mimic sunlight, and this invokes your brain to emit serotonin, a feel-good hormone. Studies show that the utilization of light therapy in times when daylight hours are short—the winter and fall—can help regulate your circadian rhythm, helping you better regulate your sleeping cycle.[71]

Energy-Healing Therapy

Focus and send yourself healing energy, vibrations, and light. Use or learn Reiki.

Reiki is a Japanese technique of healing touch that promotes relaxation and health. Together, Rei, or spiritual wisdom, and Ki, or life energy, combine to make Reiki, spiritually conscious life force energy.

Ki, also called Chi, Prana, or, in science, a Biofield, is the nonphysical energy that all living things produce. This energy leaves the living thing when it dies. Ki, life energy, flows through each of the energetic pathways of your body—your chakras, meridians, and aura—into your organs, tissues, and cells. When this flow is negatively affected, energetic blockages occur, meaning the organs, tissues, and cells of your physical body decrease in function, and subsequently illness and disease appear.

Your Ki consists of your mental, emotional, physical, and spiritual bodies. Reiki works to replace unhealthy thoughts, emotions, and vibrations with healthy and positive ones.[72]

> *"Reiki clears, straightens and heals the energetic pathways of the body, causing negative energy to break apart, burn up, melt or fall away, and allowing healthy Ki to flow naturally. Ki then flows smoothly and steadily into the organs, tissues and cells of the body, enabling them to function properly and healthily."*
> -ICAR

Reiki is used as a healing method all over the world, including in over 800 hospitals in the US alone. Hospital studies have shown Reiki to lower pain, nausea, anxiety, and recovery time after surgery, improve attitude, memory, self-confidence, and sleep, and heal trauma. Reiki helps physically by lowering aches and pains and raising mobility. Reiki helps mentally and emotionally by lowering anxiety and depression and inducing serenity, inner peace, and focus. Reiki helps spiritually by improving your relationship with your higher self, your connection to your Higher Power, and feelings of oneness with all.[73]

Acu-Therapy

Learn or receive acupressure or acupuncture.
Learn about a holistic chiropractor.

Acupuncture is a method that balances the flow of energy or life force, called "chi," that flows through the pathways, or meridians, of your body. The 12 major meridians in your body connect organ networks, streamlining them into a system of communication that runs throughout your body. When a meridian is blocked or out of balance, this can result in illness. Acupressure and acupuncture rebalance your body's channels of energy and regulate the opposing forces of yin, or feminine energy, and yang, masculine energy. Acupuncture involves inserting needles into specific points along your meridians according to the balance needed by your body and chi. Acupuncture has been shown to treat pain, provide overall wellness, lower stress, reduce chemotherapy-induced and postoperative nausea and vomiting, and reduce dental pain, headaches, labor pain, lower back pain, neck pain, osteoarthritis, and respiratory disorders, such as certain allergies.[74]

Acupressure is essentially acupuncture without the needles, but instead using your fingers to target acupressure points, and has been shown to reduce nausea, help mitigate symptoms and causes of cancer, reduce pain, treat arthritis, and lower depression and anxiety.[75]

Massage Therapy

Massage refers to rubbing and manipulating your skin and muscles.

Try different types of massage, such as Swedish massage, deep tissue massage, sports massage, and trigger point massage.

The benefits of massage include lower stress, muscle tension, heart rate and blood pressure, as well as raised levels of relaxation, circulation, energy and immune function.

Massage may also be helpful in dealing with anxiety, digestive issues, headaches, insomnia, and nerve pain.[76]

Individual and Group Therapy

Learn about

> Cognitive Behavioral Therapy
> Somatic Therapy
> Existential Therapy
> In- or Outpatient Therapy
> Family Therapy
> Couples Therapy

Seeking help from a mental health expert has been shown to help you view thoughts, feelings, and worries without judging them, create coping strategies, increase self-awareness, promote positive habit building, improve relationships, create insights, empower you, increase healthy choices, manage distress, resolve conflict, restore trust, restore intimacy, help with anxiety disorders, bipolar disorder, depression, eating disorders, substance abuse and addiction, obsessive-compulsive disorder, phobias, and post-traumatic stress disorder.[77]

Animal Therapy

Animal therapy refers to using animals to help people deal with and overcome certain physical or mental health conditions.

Interacting with a friendly animal can enhance your human-animal bond, a bond that has been shown to produce a calming state in the person. Animal therapy has been shown to lower pain levels, improve motor and social skills, lower anxiety and stress, and provide motivation. It has been shown to help with dementia, depression, anxiety, autism spectrum disorder, attention deficit hyperactivity disorder (ADHD), schizophrenia, PTSD, epilepsy, and pain from cancer treatment. Dog assisted therapy in long-term elderly care facilities has been shown to lower depression and raise social interaction and positive emotions.[78]

Inner Child Therapy

Embrace, cherish, and parent the inner child within you.
Ask what they need now.

Repeat affirmations to your inner child around their needs.

1. I am safe.
2. I am loveable.
3. I can be seen.
4. I can be heard.
6. I can make mistakes.

Engage with other people's inner child to invoke love, shift perspective, reduce animosity, and forgive.

Inner child work incorporates the psychologies of attachment theory, somatic body-based therapies, Jungian shadow work, Internal Family Systems, and psychodynamic theories, stemming from the foundation that our past experiences influence our present. When you are triggered and don't understand why, it can be your "inner child" needing attention, love, or healing. As children, we learned certain ways to keep us safe in our environments, yet frequently those behaviors no longer serve us later in life. Inner child work can create safer relationships and healthier emotional and physical states, develop a compassionate "inner parent," help you set healthy boundaries, be assertive, properly grieve a childhood or childhood experience you did not understand before, and create fun and growth as you learn to express your authentic self. Certain methods of inner child work include making room for unstructured time such as play, a craft, or a nap, checking in with your foundational physiological needs such as when you last ate or how you slept, dancing and singing to songs from your childhood or teenage years, engaging with something that provides comfort, like a cozy blanket, soft socks, sunshine, or a hug, or writing letters to yourself at a childhood age.[79]

NOURISHMENT

Food or Beverage

Food provides nutrients, which provide the energy that enables the healthy functions, activity, and growth of your body.

Enjoy eating nourishing, "real" food and beverages, like organic vegetables, fruits, nuts, seeds, purified water, and teas.

Read what the ingredients are in food and on packages.

Avoid food with ingredients that contain chemical compounds you cannot pronounce. If you don't know what an ingredient is, meaning it is not a real food, it may be best to avoid ingesting it.

Avoid toxins, which can be found in foods and environments, in order to maintain the optional performance of your body in a plethora of ways.

Wholesome, real foods have been shown to help you live longer, promote skin, teeth, eye, and muscle health, strengthen immunity and bones, reduce heart disease, type 2 diabetes, and cancers, promote healthy pregnancy, promote healthy digestive system function, and help maintain a healthy weight.[80]

Water

Engage with the healing properties of water.
Let it wash away your emotions and your thoughts.
Let it cleanse and soothe you.

Take a bath.
Take a hot shower.
Drink water.
Look at water in a glass, in the ocean, or in a river.

Your human body is composed of 60 percent water. Drinking eight eight-ounce glasses of water per day has been shown to increase physical performance, increase energy levels and brain function, prevent and treat headaches, relieve constipation, treat kidney stones, prevent hangovers, and aid in weight loss.[81]

Spend time in a float tank.
A sensory deprivation tank is a dark, soundproof pod filled with water and large amounts of salt, creating natural buoyancy. This results in restricted environmental stimulation therapy (REST).

Flotation-REST has been scientifically shown to decrease fatigue-depression, pain, stress, and anxiety, and increase energy, happiness, well-being, peace, and serenity.[82]

Integrative Health

Learn about functional medicine practitioners.

A functional medicine doctor uses holistic methods and takes into account the entire picture of your physical, mental, emotional, and spiritual health to get to the root causes of diseases and disfunction, honoring your bio-individuality. Functional medicine uses evidence-based alternative medicine to enhance your body's natural ability to repair and heal itself. It has been shown to raise health and well-being and prevent illness and disease. Functional medicine treats the person and the causes underlying their illness, as opposed to simply putting a band-aid over the symptoms without healing their root causes. This improves your quality of life by balancing hormones, improving your immunity, balancing gut health and inflammation, improving nutrition, vitamin, and mineral levels, and reducing toxins. It takes into account your physical, emotional, mental, and spiritual well-being and your biological, behavioral, psychosocial, and environmental attributes, and tailors remedies to you and your needs specifically. Functional medicine ties in Eastern medicine, including Ayurvedic herbs and botanicals used medicinally for thousands of years.[83]

Environment

Create a safe, clean space in your home environment.

Every object carries energy.
Clear your space of objects that you no longer need,
no longer want,
that no longer serve you,
or that no longer bring you joy.

Donate what you remove from your space. In this way, you make room for the receiving of new objects that are in alignment with you currently.

Declutter your home in order to help declutter your mind and help you focus and maintain clarity in your life.

> *"Outer order contributes to inner calm."*
> -GRETCHEN RUBEN

Travel

Take a short day-trip, a weekend trip, or a long trip.

Travel alone or with other people.

Take the time you travel to connect to your soul, your inner child, nature, or other people.

Travel removes you from your habitual thoughts and patterns, opens your mind up to new ways of thinking and living, and gives you fresh perspective.

> *"Not all those who wander are lost."*
> -J.R.R TOLKIEN

ENTERTAINMENT

Music

Allow yourself to be carried away by music.

Music has been shown in studies to raise mood levels, lower pain, depression, anxiety, and stress, allow you to express yourself emotionally, increase function following degenerative neurologic disorders, lower heart rate, blood pressure, and cortisol levels, and raise serotonin, endorphin, and dopamine levels.[84]

Try listening to binaural beats for relaxation and healing. Binaural beats use certain pulsing sounds to align your brain waves to the frequency of the beat being played. These have been shown to enhance focus, relaxation, and sleep, and lower anxiety and pain.[85]

Try listening to Solfeggio Frequencies for relaxation and healing. Solfeggio Frequencies are seven sound tones that are derived from numerology and have been used for healing for centuries.

These specific frequencies can positively shift the vibrations of theindividuals and environment in which they are played. The 396 Hz Solfeggio Frequency can remove feelings of guilt, help overcome fear, empower your goals, and help balance your root chakra. The 417 Hz Solfeggio Frequency can remove negative energy from your body, home, and environment, remove negative thought patterns from your mind, and help you change and balance your sacral chakra. The 528 Hz Solfeggio Frequency can reduce stress, bring about transformation, increase self-confidence, and balance your solar plexus chakra. The 639 Hz Solfeggio Frequency can create harmony in your relationships, encourage healthy cell communication, enhance love and tolerance, and balance your heart chakra. The 741 Hz Solfeggio Frequency can clean your cells, remove toxins, clear electromagnetic radiation, and balance your throat chakra. The 852 Hz Solfeggio Frequency can aid your intuition, inner strength, spirituality, and balance your third eye chakra. The 963 Hz Solfeggio Frequency can create "cellular enlightenment," transforming your cells to a higher level, create feelings of oneness, and balance your crown chakra.[86]

Listen to Solfeggio Frequencies online and note how you feel beforeand after.

Movie or Show

Enjoy a film or series.

Cinema therapy, or movie therapy, where individuals watch movies based on their current issues, has been shown to lower negative thoughts and bad habits and increase one's ability to manage their life. Watching comedies, or any movie that causes you to laugh for fifteen minutes, dilates your blood vessels by 22 percent, which lowers your blood pressure and reduces stress. Watching sad movies has been shown to boost endorphin release. Watching horror movies has been shown to raise white blood cell production, which is key in fighting disease. Movies have been shown to help us pause from reality and cope with stress. They unite families and friends, give us inspiration, learning, and creativity, and help us deal with life events.[87]

Book

Curl up with a book.

Studies show that regular reading increases brain connectivity, improves comprehension, improves vocabulary, increases levels of empathy, helps sleep, lowers stress, blood pressure, and heart rate, lowers symptoms of depression, defends against cognitive decline brought on by aging, and helps you live a longer life.[88]

IN CASE OF EMERGENCY

IT HAPPENED. YOU ARE TRIGGERED. Perhaps you feel angry, frustrated, anxious, or depressed. No matter how or why you find yourself upset, and no matter who or what upset you, you are best served by choosing to self-regulate at this point. The benefits of this choice to your personal health, as well as the health of your relationships, are numerous. Your application of self-regulation techniques also trains these muscles to respond in the future. This creates new and better equipped pathways in your brain and emotional response systems.

Start by checking in with your physical body. Note what may be happening automatically as a result of being triggered. Is your breathing rapid, your heart rate elevated, your blood pressure raised, your muscles shaking, your pupils dilated, or your skin flushed? If so, acknowledge that your fight-or-flight response has kicked in, and pause.

Wait twenty to sixty minutes for your body chemistry to reset to where it was before you were triggered before you take action, such as replying or responding to whom or what triggered you.

During this time, talk to your body and redirect the automated processes that may be occurring inside of you. "Amygdala, I am safe. I don't need you to initiate my fight-or-flight response. Limbic system, I know that you are trying to protect me, but I don't need that archaic form of protection today. I can access my prefrontal cortex now and return to a calm and stable state. I am safe."

Take a full, long, deep breath. Lower your heart rate and blood pressure by invoking your parasympathetic nervous system and your vagus nerve. Breath slowly to signal your body to relax and release toxins. Inhale and stretch your stomach open, and exhale by contracting your stomach muscles. Breathe in your nose for four counts, pause for four counts, breathe out your mouth for eight counts, and pause for four counts. Vocalize your breath. Breathe in your nose and mouth for eight counts and breathe out your nose and mouth for ten counts. Breathe in as long and fully as you can, and breathe out as long and fully as you can. Inhale everything new, and exhale everything old.

Engage with your senses to redirect your experience. Tune into hearing, your fastest sense. Listen to the sounds around you, near and far, and label them. Name five things you can see, four things you can touch, three things you can hear, two things you can smell, and one thing you can taste.

Mentally scan your body. Relax your temples and your jaw. Move your attention slowly through each part of your body, from your toes, to your legs, to your core, to your arms, to the top of your head. Observe how the different areas of your body feel.

Next, check in with your mental experience. Accept what you are thinking, investigate where it appears in your body—perhaps your gut is clenched or your throat is tight—and then detach from and release the thought itself. Notice whether you are hungry, angry, lonely, or tired, and recognize that these states can affect your perception of events. Remember that everyone in life is experiencing their own difficulties and know that you are free to choose not to take whatever is happening in your experience personally.

You are the leader of your thoughts, so guide your thoughts wisely in the direction that best serves you. Feed the good wolf inside of you, connecting with peace, kindness, love, and faith. Spiral up with your thoughts, pondering on best-case scenarios. What if things go other than you planned and still turn out alright? What if there was one scenario that you had not yet imagined where this all ends up okay? What if everything is happening for your ultimate well-being?

Practice radical acceptance to reduce suffering, knowing that you can identify something as true without agreeing with it. Ask yourself if you really need to shoot the second arrow at yourself, or if you can experience a state of no wind and enjoy the nirvana that comes from viewing life with no distortions.

Let go of judging others or yourself. You don't need to constantly decide whether you approve or disapprove of something. You can experience things outright instead of adding this burden to everything.

If you notice your thoughts are straying toward thoughts of the past or future, let go of those thoughts and direct your focus to the present moment. Picture thoughts floating across the sky of your mind as passing, puffy clouds. Look to birds as a prime example of living in the present, as they neither regret the past nor fear future, yet they are provided for. Ask yourself, "Can I be here now?" Affirm, "I can."

Flex your equanimity muscles and neither push against nor pull toward your experience. Instead of extrapolating about the future, say to yourself, "We'll see." Embrace silence by "thinking" about stillness and inner peace, and visualizing silence taking over your mind.

Check in with your emotional body and bring in self-care. Imagine what your friendly inner support system would say at this moment. "I love you! You are doing a great job! The Universe adores you!" Acknowledge that you are doing your best. Even if things are not going how you want them to, validate that you are doing the very best you can with the tools and the knowledge that you have. Know that your intentions are what you can control, not outcomes, so release expectations for specific results and focus on your part in things. Let go of perfectionism. It is not attainable and never was meant to be. No longer expect perfectionism from yourself or others. Recognize the plethora of health problems that result from perfectionistic tendencies as motivation to disengage with these tendencies.

Remember that without caring for yourself, you cannot properly care for others. Focus on yourself and your ability to experience life, grow, and create. Show yourself compassionate nurturing, tenderness, kindness, and gentleness. Speak to yourself as if you are your own child, best friend, or romantic partner. Run your thoughts through the lens of "Am I being nice to myself?" If your current thought is not a kind one, let go of it and allow a new, more compassionate one.

Check in with whose voice you are prioritizing mentally. Does the voice sound like a rendition of someone who has judged or criticized you in the past? Let go of the negative voices that are not yours, and picture what the positive voice of your friend, family member, therapist, pet, Inner Being, or Higher Power would lovingly say to you at this time.

Keep your focus on yourself. Thinking about other people and their thoughts, words, or actions is futile, as you cannot control other people, and what other people think about you is not your business. Stay in your metaphorical hula hoop and repeat the serenity prayer to help you do so.

Enjoy being authentically you. Yours is the only opinion that matters when it comes to how you feel about yourself. Avoid letting yourself be swayed by what other people expect from you. Make decisions based on how you feel instead of how other people may feel. Let go of caring what anyone else thinks. Validate yourself from within, resonating with the fact that you have nothing to prove to anyone.

Recognize that other people's judgements are about them, not you. Forgive yourself and others, liberating yourself from the toxic emotions of hate and resentment that only hurt the person feeling them.

Build your self-trust by noting your choices of well-being, both big and small. Choosing to self-regulate by doing these exercises is cause alone for increasing your self-trust. Acknowledge that being vulnerable and open is for your greatest good, even if you incur pain sometimes along the way. Communicate your feelings and thoughts in love and kindness, neither in aggression nor in silence. If you choose to communicate at this time, pause during the conversation if you feel triggered, actively listen to the other person, engage with the other person's inner child, orient to solutions, and call in any appropriate outside help that you have available to you.

Go slow and steady. Be easy on yourself and rest when you can. What is the easiest thing you could think about as it relates to this scenario? What is the easiest thing you could do?

Look to nature for help with whatever you are going through. Know that you are meant to let go of toxic emotions, thoughts, and people, shedding in the same way a tree does each fall. Look to butterflies to build trust in your stages of growth and universal timing. Note how many animals access dimensions to vision that we as humans don't access, and use this concept to connect with the nonphysical energies of your Higher Power that may be helpful to you.

Check in with your patterns of thoughts, emotions, speech, nourishment, and sleep in order to recognize where you are now and where you want to be in relation to these areas. Acknowledge that the more balanced each of these areas are, the more balanced you are overall, and the more clarity you have in challenging situations.

View pain as the teacher it is and recognize it as an opportunity for growth. Accept pain, forgive it, forgive yourself for holding onto it and appreciate how you grew from it. Then, release it. Recognize the part you played in past stories, recognize that you are no longer a part of those stories, release them, and fill yourself with your natural bright light. View pain as happening for you, not to you.

Watch events, feelings, and sensations from the place of the witness and neutral observer. Imagine if this was your last moment on Earth and how this would change your actions. Since you never know when you will transition, live the life you would want to live if it were your last opportunity to do so. Remember that everything is temporary, and everything passes eventually, and so will this. View your life as a chemistry experiment. Try things out, watch what happens, and adjust accordingly. What could currently be seen as negative may eventually help you know more of what you do want, from which knowledge you can make a better life for yourself.

Take things one day at a time, one thing at a time, bird by bird. If you feel that you can't do something, try affirming, "I can." Believe in the impossible. Be proud of yourself for showing up, and keep showing up for yourself. Embrace the pivot and blend, turning away from what you don't want and turning toward what you do want. Try doing the opposite of what you've been doing if you aren't getting the results you wanted, just as an experiment. Know that as you pivot away from what no longer serves you, things may feel tumultuous, so focus on your alignment with your Higher Power, let the changes unfold, and allow your life to transform into the life you have always wanted. If you feel unduly tested, continue to face each challenge head on and watch as you may reach new heights and new rewards may await you.

Focus on the positive aspects of yourself, your environment, your day, and your life. Find these everywhere you go, as if your life is one big positive-aspect treasure hunt.

Check in with your spiritual state. Breathe into your energy centers, your chakras, to balance them. Breathe in and out of your root chakra and adrenals, rise to your sacral chakra and reproductive organs, move to your solar plexus and pancreas, your heart chakra and thymus gland, your throat chakra and thyroid, your third eye chakra and pituitary gland, and finally your crown chakra and pineal gland. Breathe into your lower body, upper body, front body, back body, and entire body as a whole.

Set your future in motion with the choices you make now. If you want to increase your self-mastery and self-regulation, choose to engage in those activities now, and be proud of yourself for doing so. Think and speak in a way that accurately reflects who you want to be and where you want to be, as your thoughts and speech are energetic vibrations that you send out to the Universe, and the Universe responds in kind.

Think downstream thoughts, such as "you can do it, strong cells." Tell any bodily discomfort you are experiencing that you love it in order to reduce resistance to it, and thereby allow well-being more quickly. Recognize that all feelings and thoughts are temporary, so this sensation, like any other, shall pass—just like it has in the past.

Recognize what you are in control of as it pertains to your energy. Empower yourself by affirming that you are confidently in control of your voice, your feet, your eyes, your ears, your emotions, your thoughts, your choices, and your action or inaction in all environments. Channel the energy you wish to align with, whatever that may be, including feminine, masculine, child, solution, divine, and unification consciousness energy.

Detach from any negative thought bubbles that are in your experience and shine the light of consciousness on any resulting negative emotions or feelings of discomfort in order to transmute them into positive energy.

Engage in activities that lower your stress and increase your well-being. Meditate or journal. Move by skipping, running, doing jumping jacks, or dancing. Cover your nose, cheeks, eyes, and forehead with a cold washcloth, an ice pack, or put your face directly in cold water to initiate your Mammalian Dive Response. Reset your cranial nerve. Activate your autonomous sensory meridian response. Utilize the emotional freedom technique, EFT, or tapping. Earth by walking barefoot outside. Scream it out. Scream loud and long into a pillow or out in nature.

Try different forms of therapy including aromatherapy, sound therapy, crystal therapy, chromotherapy, seasonal affective disorder therapy, energy healing therapy, acu-therapy, massage therapy, professional therapy, animal therapy, or inner child therapy.

Nurture yourself with nourishment. Eat real food and beverages. Drink water or take a shower. See an integrative health practitioner.

Distract yourself with music, including binaural beats and Solfeggio Frequencies. See a movie, show, or read a book. Reach out and call a friend, family member, therapist, or join a support group.

Give all your worries up to your Higher Power. Envision your concerns in balloons or write them down and release them to your Higher Power, turning them over completely and leaving them safely in their care.

Defer to the wisdom and expertise of the Universe. Trust in the natural order of the Universe, and avoid obsessing over the clock and the calendar, and changing your mood based on the day of the week. Let today feel like Saturday, if you please.

Align yourself to the rhythm of the Universe by syncing each step you take to a musical beat. Relish the dance of life, eloquently grasping the hand of a new partner, place, or thing, and gracefully letting go of the hand of a past one, all the while honoring the time you spend dancing alone.

View life from a broad perspective. One million years from now, what will matter? Envision how you'll feel in one week, one month, one year, or one lifetime from now.

Ask your Inner Being, the best version of you and your highest self, to guide you in all things. If you don't want to do something you feel is necessary, show up and channel your Inner Being, and let them complete the task through you. Connect to what the best version of you would do right now. Summon forth and invoke love, well-being, kindness, your Higher Power, and your highest self.

Focus on today and right now. Be a blank canvas every day and every moment. Let go of past programmings, past stories, and past events. Let go of what happened yesterday and what may happen tomorrow.

Envision being one with all other life. Become aware that you are consciousness living in your vessel, just as other humans, animals, and plants are consciousness living in their vessels. Remove the differentiating factors of the vessel you are in, and connect to what unites you. Resonate internally with harmony, joy, and laughter. Then, look for these traits in others, and you may be surprised how easily you find them.

Just as the wind creates shores, practice balancing your body, mind, and spirit continuously, and little by little, over time, balance may just become your inherent state of being.

"You can be fully satisfied with where you are, understanding that you're eternally evolving. When you get into that place of feeling appreciation of where you are and of who you are, and appreciation of what you are, and you accept that you are a never-ending, always unfolding Being, then you can stand in that delicate balance of being optimistic about what is to come, without being unhappy about where you stand. Find a way of eagerly anticipating future changes, while at the same time you are in love and satisfied with who, what, where and how you be."
    -ABRAHAM-HICKS

"I choose who I am becoming,
and I run towards it
with conviction and consistent motion."
    -CHRIS-ANNE DONELLY

"Peace. It does not mean to be in a place where there is no noise, trouble, or hard work. It means to be in the midst of those things and still be calm in your heart."
    -UNKNOWN

"There is freedom waiting for you
on the breezes of the sky
And you ask, 'What if I fall?'
'Oh but my darling, what if you fly?'"
    -ERIN HANSON

ABOUT THE AUTHOR

LUCY BYRD HOPE IS A holistic guide, spiritualist, and entrepreneur who received her BA in Psychology from the University of Texas at Austin. Lucy built onto this foundation by learning cognitive behavioral, somatic, and existential psychology as well as alternative medicine. She initially became certified in Mindfulness-Based Stress Reduction at Duke Integrative Medicine. To further her education in holistic medicine, Lucy received her Reiki Level I, Level II, and Master certifications. She has also received her first and second level Shamanic Mastery certifications and is currently completing her third level Mastery.

As an entrepreneur, Lucy has successfully started multiple businesses. Currently, she operates LucYd Lotus, an energy wellness company, and Wholism, a plant-based beverage company focused on bringing nutritional function and awareness to consumers.

On any given day, you can find Lucy connecting with nature, bonding with animals, writing, dreaming up new business ideas, traveling, exploring, and adventuring into the unknown!

ENDNOTES

1. Elaine N. Aron, *The Highly Sensitive Person*, Broadway Books, June 2, 1997.

2. Daniel Goleman, *Emotional Intelligence: Why It Can Matter More Than IQ*, Random House Publishing Group, September 27, 2005.

3. Ito TA, Larsen JT, Smith NK, Cacioppo JT, "Negative information weighs more heavily on the brain: the negativity bias in evaluative categorizations," *J Pers Soc Psychol*, Oct 1998, https://doi.org/ 10.1037//0022-3514.75.4.887.

4. National Science Foundation, https://nsf.gov.

5. Seth S. Horowitz, "The Science and Art of Listening," *NY Times*, Nov 9, 2012. Seth S. Horowitz, *The Universal Sense: How Hearing Shapes the Mind*, Bloomsbury USA, August 20, 2013.

6. Luis Villazon, "What is the time resolution of our senses," *BBC Science Focus Magazine*.

7. Gretchen Cuda, "Just Breathe: Body Has A Built-In Stress Reliever," *NPR*, December 6, 2010.

8. Andrea Watkins, LCSW, "Benefits of Deep Breathing," *Urban Balance*, November 3, 2014.

9. Isabelle Pikörn, "The 5-4-3-2-1 Grounding Technique: Manage Anxiety By Anchoring In The Present," *Insight Timer Blog*.

10. Jessica Caporuscio, "Grounding techniques: Step-by-step guide and methods," *Medical News Today*, March 31, 2020.

11. B Grace Bullock, PhD, "How the Body Scan Meditation Practice Reduces Biological Stress," January 9, 2020, mindful.org.

12. Michael Stone, "Powerful Emotions and S.A.I.N.," February 19, 2013, michaelstoneteaching.com.

13. "Hope from My Very First Meeting," Al-Anon Family Groups, August 2018, https://al-anon.org/blog/hope-from-my-very-first-meeting/.

14. Pilar Gerasimo, "Emotional Biochemistry," *Experience Life*, November 1, 2020.

15. Kendra Cherry, "How the Fight or Flight Response Works," August 18, 2019, stress.org

16. Sarah Hodges, "Triggered? Find Power in the Pause," November 14, 2018, hodgescoaching.com

17. Pilar Gerasimo, "Emotional Biochemistry," *Experience Life*, November 1, 2020.

What Is An Anxiety Spiral?," *Insight Timer Blog*

₃y, "Non-Judgment: What is it? And Why Does it Matter? (4 Benefits)," *Ambition*

..art Tolle, *The Power of Now: A Guide to Spiritual Enlightenment*, Namaste ₂ublishing, 1997.

1. Matt. 5-7, "The Sermon on the Mount."

22. Courtney E. Ackerman, MA, "How to Live in the Present Moment: 35 Exercises and Tools (+ Quotes)," *Positive Psychology*, October 22, 2018.

23. Buddhist Parable

24. "This Buddhist Parable Can Ease Your Suffering During a Crisis," *Big Think*, June 27, 2017.

25. "This Buddhist Parable Can Ease Your Suffering During a Crisis," *Big Think*, June 27, 2017.

26. Julie Mann, Chinese Proverb adaptation

27. Dr. Munr Kazmir, "We'll See," *Medium*, October 8, 2020.

28. Parisha Jijina, Urmi Nanda Biswas, "Understanding equanimity from a psychological perspective: implications for holistic well-being during a global pandemic," *Taylor & Francis Online*, November 4, 2021.

29. Gaëlle Desbordes, Tim Gard, Elizabeth A. Hoge, Britta K. Hölzel, Catherine Kerr, Sara W. Lazar, Andrew Olendzki, David R. Vago, "Moving beyond Mindfulness: Defining Equanimity as an Outcome Measure in Meditation and Contemplative Research," *Mindfulness (N Y)* (January 2014): 356-372, https://doi.org/ 10.1007/ s12671-013-0269-8.

30. Healthwise Staff, "Stop Negative Thoughts: Choosing a Healthier Way of Thinking," *HealthLinkBC*, June 16, 2021.

31. Deepak Chopra, MD, "Only a Silent Mind Can Be a Healing Mind," *Chopra*, March 30, 2020.

32. Serena Chen, "Give Yourself a Break: The Power of Self-Compassion," *Harvard Business Review*, September-October 2018.

33. Amanda Ruggeri, "The dangerous downsides of perfectionism," *BBC*, February 20, 2018.

34. "The Benefits Of Self-Compassion And How To Get More," *The Best Brain Possible*, June 26, 2016.

35. Michael A. Singer, *The Untethered Soul: The Journey Beyond Yourself*, New Harbinger Publications/Noetic Books, October 3, 2007.

36. GTTG Team, "Self-Compassion: Becoming Your Inner Ally," *GT Therapy*, May 29, 2019.

37. "Critical Inner Voice," PsychAlive.

38. Henry, "8 Ways to Focus on Yourself and Not Others (With Examples)," *Tracking Happiness*, August 6, 2022.

39. Kimanzi Constable, "Why Making Yourself a Priority Boosts Your Productiv *Lifehack*, July 12, 2021.

40. Paulina Xenia, "Being Unapologetically You: Why It's So Healing to Your Soul and Hov Breath Work Can Help," *Human Amplified*.

41. Brené Brown, *8 Benefits of Being Vulnerable that Will Improve your Life*.

42. Kendra Cherry, "How the Fight or Flight Response Works," *The American Institute of Stress*, August 18, 2019.

43. WebMD Editorial Contributors, Dan Brennan, MD, "Setting Boundaries," *WebMD*, October 25, 2021.

44. *Queens of Mystery*, Julian Unthank, April 8, 2019, *BBC*.

45. Dr. Jolene Brighten, "What Are the Benefits of Gratitude for Your Hormones and Health?," December 5, 2021.

46. "How to Pivot in Your Career and Life, According to an Empowerment Coach," *Create & Cultivate*, August 24, 2020.

47. Anne-Laure Le Cunff, "An ode to slowness: the benefits of slowing down," *Ness Labs*.

48. Kathy Kruger, "Why Slow is the Way to Go: 6 Reasons to Take Your Time," *Tiny Buddha*.

49. Lao Tzu, *Tao Te Ching*, Penguin Classics, May 30, 1964.

50. Michael A. Singer, *The Untethered Soul: The Journey Beyond Yourself*, New Harbinger Publications/Noetic Books, October 3, 2007.

51. "The Observer Meditation," *Positive Psychology*.

52. "The Lessons of Nature," *The School of Life*.

53. 11 Benefits of Chakra Meditation February 17, 2016 By admin Relaxation Meditation, Wellness & Health.

54. Eckhart Tolle, *The Power of Now: A Guide to Spiritual Enlightenment*, Namaste Publishing, 1997.

55. Esther Hicks, *Abraham-Hicks Publications*.

56. Mayo Clinic Staff, "Meditation: A simple, fast way to reduce stress," *Mayo Clinic*, April 29, 2022.

57. Nooria Khan, "5 Science-Backed Benefits Of Journaling," *CreateWriteNow*, November 18, 2019.

58. Mayo Clinic Staff, "Exercise and stress: Get moving to manage stress," *Mayo Clinic*, August 3, 2022.

59. Stig Severinsen, "The Diving Reflex," *Breathology*.

60. Stanley Rosenberg, *Accessing the Healing Power of the Vagus Nerve: Self-Help Exercises for Anxiety, Depression, Trauma, and Autism*, North Atlantic Books, December 5, 2017.

61. Matthew Whittle, "ASMR and Sleep," January 7, 2022.

62. *The Tapping Solution*

63. Church, 2012.

64. *The Tapping Solution*

65. Wendy Menigoz, Tracy T. Latz, Robin A. Ely, Cimone Kamei, Gregory Melvin, Drew Sinatra, "Integrative and lifestyle medicine strategies should include Earthing

eview of research evidence and clinical observations," *Explore*, Volume (May–June 2020): 152-160.

ronkleton, "Aromatherapy Uses and Benefits," *Healthline*, March 8, 2019.

y Whelan, "The 15 Best Essential Oils to Try," *Healthline*, February 26, 2020.

adrienne Santos-Longhurst , "The Uses and Benefits of Music Therapy," *Audiotherapy*, January 27, 2020.

69. TNN, "The science behind healing crystals explained!," *Entertainment Times of India*, Aug 1, 2019.

70. Samina T. Yousuf Azeemi, S. Mohsin Raza "A Critical Analysis of Chromotherapy and Its Scientific Evolution," *Evid Based Complement Alternat Med* (December 2005): 481-488.

71. Corey Whelan, "5 Best SAD Lamps for Seasonal Affective Disorder and How to Use Them," *Healthline*, October 28, 2021.

72. *International Center for Reiki Training (ICRT)*.

73. *International Center for Reiki Training (ICRT)*.

74. *Acupuncture Mayo Clinic*.

75. Annie Stuart, "Acupressure Points and Massage Treatment," *WebMD*, October 31, 2021.

76. Mayo Clinic Staff, "Massage: Get in touch with its many benefits," *Mayo Clinic*, January 12, 2021.

77. Sara Lindberg, "Benefits and Options for Therapy," *Healthline*, October 23, 2020.

78. Jon Johnson, "What to know about animal therapy," *Medical News Today*, July 10, 2020.

79. "What is Inner Child Work?," *Psyche and Soma*, March 19, 2021.

80. "Benefits of Healthy Eating," *CDC*, May 16, 2021.

81. Joe Leech, "7 Science-Based Health Benefits of Drinking Enough Water Written," *Healthline*, June 30, 2020.

82. Justin S. Feinstein, Sahib S. Khalsa, Hung-Wen Yeh, Colleen Wohlrab, W. Kyle Simmons, Murray B. Stein, Martin P. Paulus, "Examining the short-term anxiolytic and antidepressant effect of Floatation-REST," *PLoS One* (February 2018).

83. "Six benefits of integrative medicine," *Honor Health*.

84. "9 Health Benefits of Music," *NorthShore University HealthSystem*, December 31, 2020.

85. Adrienne Santos-Longhurst, "The Uses and Benefits of Music Therapy," *Audiotherapy*, January 27, 2020.

86. "Benefits of Music based on 7 Solfeggio Frequencies," *Meditative Mind*.

87. "10 benefits of watching movies," *BREO BOX*, June 22, 2020.

88. Rebecaa Joy Stanborough, "Benefits of Reading Books: How It Can Positively Affect Your Life Medically," *Thrive*, October 15, 2019.